Cleman Mountain and elk at Oak Creek feeding station

WILDLIFE AREAS OF WASHINGTON

Text by Susan Schwartz
Photographs by Bob and Ira Spring
Maps by Marge Mueller

Superior PUBLISHING COMPANY

Acknowledgment

The author and photographers wish to thank the personnel of the U.S. Fish and Wildlife Service, the Washington State Department of Game and the National Park Service for the encouragement and help they received on this guide book.

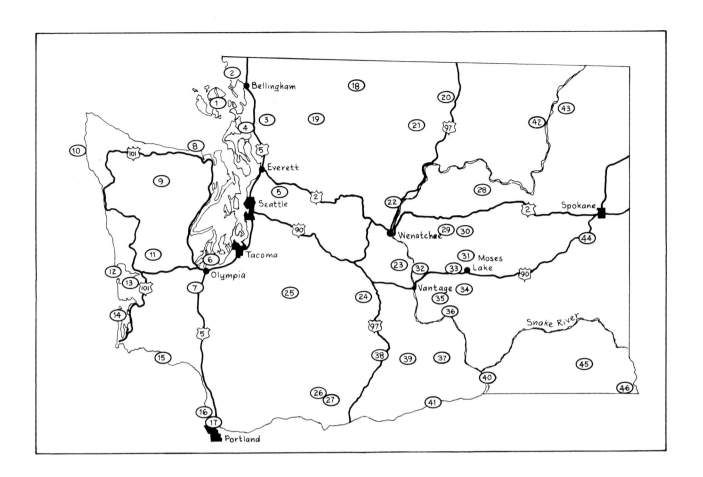

Library of Congress Cataloging in Publication Data

Spring, Bob and Ira, 1918-
Washington wild life areas.

Includes index.
1. Natural history—Washing-
ton (State)—Pictorial works.
2. Wilderness areas—Washing-
ton (State) — Pictorial works.
I. Spring, Ira.
II. Schwartz, Susan.
III. Title.
QH105.W2S67 574.9791'022'2 76-16159
ISBN 0-87564-623-9

FIRST EDITION

PRINTED AND BOUND IN THE UNITED STATES OF AMERICA

KEY TO WILDLIFE AREAS
OF WASHINGTON

Washington State Game Department's
Wildlife Recreation Areas are often referred to
as W.R.A.

FOREWORD

This guide book is intended to show people something of the wide variety of wildlife living on publicly-owned lands in Washington—and to tell readers how they can enjoy this wildlife while leaving it undisturbed as possible.

Those who set out to use this guide to watch birds and animals should remember that they owe a great deal of thanks to hunters, here and across the country, for many of these birds and animals even being there. As wildlife was slaughtered and its living habitat wiped out as "civilization" spread across our continent, it was primarily hunters who goaded Congress and state lawmakers into enacting wildlife-conservation laws. Hunters' fees paid for game lands and the wages of people that manage them.

Hunters are still in the forefront of wildlife conservation. The non-hunter, however, must add his voice and his dollar to the cause. There still is much to be done. And some of it may be contrary to the desires of most hunters.

Thanks to laws and regulations adopted at hunters' insistence, there is little danger of any species in this nation today being hunted to extinction. Washington may well have more wild animals today than it did 50 years ago, thanks to careful state and federal management.

But in my opinion, this state (and every state) should have one sanctuary large enough to let its major game animals live safe from hunting in all seasons of the year. And some of the scarcer game animals, such as mountain goats and big-horn sheep, should not be hunted at all.

Animals in their natural state—that is, not hunted by guns—treat humans almost as equals. Some species, such as mountain goats, bighorn sheep, and deer, are quite friendly and curious. Others, such as elk, buffalo, and bear, are wary and generally keep man at a respectful distance. Still others, such as cougar, are furtive and seldom seen whether hunted or not.

An example of this kind of year-round sanctuary is Yellowstone National Park. Here, animals can be watched up close. They seem scarcely disturbed by hikers, skiiers, tourists in cars.

The only sanctuary in Washington approaching Yellowstone's size is the Olympic National Park. Here, mountain goats, that spend winter and summer in the park and are never hunted, seem nearly as interested in hikers as hikers are in them. There are large numbers of elk in the Olympics, too. But winter takes them out of the park boundary and into range of the hunters' guns. Inside or outside the park, the elk flee from man. By contrast, in Yellowstone, elk spend their entire lives within the park boundary. They graze along park roads indifferent to tourists taking their pictures. Hikers find it advisable to make short detours around elk standing in their trails.

Bighorn sheep are another example. The journal of Captain Bonneville tells of his 1832 expedition to Idaho's Sawtooth Mountains. The bighorn sheep among the precipices there were so friendly that his men could walk up to them and easily kill as many as they pleased. Today, the Bighorns in the Sawtooths, like those in Washington, are hunted—and they flee at the sight of man. Those in Glacier and Yellowstone National Parks, protected by law, still are almost friendly.

A year-round sanctuary would be good for the species as well as pleasant for wildlife watchers. Animals generally have a social order in which the healthiest and strongest males do most of the mating. Hunting—by breaking up herds and shooting many of the prime animals—changes this natural social order and leaves many of the weaker animals to do the mating.

A California study indicated that among people who said they were interested in wildlife, 20 per cent said they wanted to hunt, and 80 per cent said they wanted to just watch living animals. This non-hunting majority should have some "game" animals left for them, to be enjoyed in their natural, non-hunted state, without even the need to travel to a wildlife sanctuary. This doesn't mean deer and elk shouldn't be hunted—They are plentiful, and if not hunted they would multiply too fast, interfere with agriculture, and be hazards on the highways. But mountain goats and bighorn sheep would be ideal protected species. They do not infringe on civilization, and it is unlikely that they would suffer from serious overpopulation if not hunted. If herds did grow too large, some animals could be removed in a way that would not terrorize the others.

Of course, these recommendations will not become reality easily, if they ever do. Hunting interests are a powerful lobby. Already squeezed out of much of their former territory, they will fight any move to create large new sanctuaries. In theory, if 80 per cent of those interested in wildlife want their share alive, organizations like the Audubon Society should be five times as large and powerful as hunting groups—but the reverse generally is true.

Those interested should support organizations that promote wildlife conservation without stressing hunting. They also should be willing to shoulder their share of the financial burden. Perhaps all who use wildlife areas should be required to purchase a hunting or non-hunting "wildlife license," just as all those who drive cars should have licenses. But the likelihood of this becoming law seems remote. And so far, efforts in various states to promote voluntary non-hunting licenses have largely failed.

Non-hunters should remember that they can harm animals as much, or more, as people with guns. Hunting today is done only when animals are in good condition and can stand the strain. The hunters stay away in winter, when animals must conserve their energy; and in the nursing season.

But skiers or snowmobilers can frighten animals into running in deep snow—an exertion that can be fatal if it happens often enough. Summertime hikers can stampede elk cows into leaving their young unfed and unprotected. They can set mountain goat nannies and kids fleeing when they should be nursing. Bird-watchers can frighten birds from their nests, leaving eggs and young vulnerable to marauding crows, gulls, and other enemies. Enough disturbance will cause birds to abandon nest, eggs, or young. And one dog brought along on a family camping trip can do as much damage to nests and to small and young animals as can several people with rifles.

So far, the restrictions needed to cut down man-wildlife conflicts like these are scattered and fairly few. Many national wildlife refuges restrict access of bird-nesting areas. Snowmobilers have been restricted in many game areas.

As the out-of-doors becomes more crowded, though, more restrictions and more compromises will be necessary. Non-hunters must be willing to shoulder their share of this burden. They might get enlarged wildlife sanctuaries. But in return, they must be willing to accept restricted use of areas in critical seasons (for example, while young are being reared). They will have to leave their dogs at home. They will have to learn to stay on trails and out of areas that may be key resting, feeding, or rearing places for animals.

by Ira Spring

ABOUT THE PHOTOGRAPHS

These photographs, mostly taken within a few short months, truly represent the larger birds and mammals anyone can see on a day's visit to the wildlife areas represented.

Some of the areas, such as Lake Terrell and Scatter Creek, were visited when their wildlife was at its quiet season. Others were visited at the peak of their wildlife show.

Generally, the pictures were taken during one visit to a specific area. But return trips were made to the Sinlahekin and W.T. Wooten Wildlife Recreation Areas to photograph the bighorn sheep that eluded the photographer on the first visit. A few areas—the national parks, the Potholes area, and the eagle sanctuary—are longtime favorites photographed many times by Bob or his twin brother, Ira.

Wild animals don't read boundary signs. All the pictures in this book were taken in the immediate vicinity of the wildlife areas, but not necessarily within the exact boundaries. The eagle and magpie sharing a road kill were photographed from the car window a mile south of Entiat W.R.A., along the Columbia. The deer in North Cascades National Park was taken on the Ptarmigan Traverse, a hike that starts in the park, at Cascade Pass, but ends outside it near Glacier Peak. The Bighorn sheep shown in the chapter on the Sinlahekin were on state land a mile outside the wildlife area. The curlew was in a farmyard near Desert Wildlife Recreation Area.

The sweeping scenics, like the flower fields at Mt. Rainier, the canyon in Asotin Wildlife Recreation Area, and the air views of the ocean; were taken with a Speed Graphic, a 4 × 5-inch view camera. The animal pictures were nearly all taken with a 2¼ × 2¾-inch Mamiya, a roll film camera using a 350 mm. lens. Except for the owl picture at Toppenish, which was too close for the big lens, the bird pictures were taken on a 35 mm. Canon with a 1,000 mm. mirror lens. The black and white pictures were all taken on Tri-X film. Most of the bird pictures were taken from inside the car, with the lens firmly braced against the open window.

This arsenal of cameras is fine when photographing from the car. On foot, however, a choice must be made of just one—and sometimes it is the wrong one. So occasionally we take a scenic with a 35 mm. camera; and the bear at Leadbetter Point should have been taken with a telephoto, but only the large scenic camera was in the pack that day.

White-crowned sparrow in the Columbian White-tailed Deer National Refuge

SOME LIKELY SPOTS FOR WILDLIFE

ELK

Olympic Natl. Park—Page 30, Colockum W.R.A.—Page 68, Oak Creek W.R.A.—Page 72, W.T. Wooten W.R.A.—Page 124. Also found on the east side of Mt. St. Helens and inland from Willapa Bay Natl. Wildlife Refuge—Page 42.

DEER

Found by twos or threes from city suburbs to mountain meadows and at the Columbia White-Tailed Deer Natl. Wildlife Refuge—Page 46. Found in large concentrations during the winter months at Sinlahekin—Page 58, Entiat Mountains—Page 64, Klickitat W.R.A.—Page 82, Pend Oreille W.R.A.—Page 118, W.T. Wooten W.R.A.—Page 124.

BIGHORN SHEEP

Sinlahekin W.R.A.—Page 58, Entiat W.R.A.—Page 64, W.T. Wooten W.R.A.—Page 124.

MOUNTAIN GOATS

Olympic Natl. Park—Page 30, Mt. Rainier Natl. Park—Page 76.

BLACK BEAR

Olympic Natl. Park—Page 30, Mt. Rainier Natl. Park—Page 76.

MARMOTS

Olympic Natl. Park—Page 30, Mt. Rainier Natl. Park—Page 76.

TRUMPETER SWANS

Trumpeter Lakes—Page 16, Turnbull Natl. Wildlife Refuge—Page 120.

WHISTLING SWANS

Skagit W.R.A.—Page 18, Turnbull Natl. Wildlife Refuge—Page 120, and anywhere along the lower Columbia River.

WHITE PELICANS

Occasionally in August. Potholes W.R.A.—Page 94, Sunnyside W.R.A.—Page 110, Columbia River near McNary W.R.A.—Page 112.

CANADA GEESE

Willapa Natl. Wildlife Refuge—Page 42, Ridgefield Natl. Wildlife Refuge—Page 48, Conboy Natl. Wildlife Refuge—Page 80, Banks Lake W.R.A.—Page 84, Long Lake W.R.A.—Page 88, Turnbull Natl. Wildlife Refuge—Page 120.

SNOW GEESE

Skagit W.R.A.—Page 18.

BLACK BRANT

Dungeness Natl. Wildlife Refuge—Page 26, Willapa Natl. Wildlife Refuge—Page 42, and throughout Puget Sound.

WOOD DUCKS

Lake Terrell W.R.A.—Page 14.

LARGE FLOCKS OF MIGRATING DUCKS

San Juan Islands—Page 12, Lake Terrell W.R.A.—Page 14, Nisqually Delta—Page 22, Ridgefield Natl. Wildlife Refuge—Page 48, Vancouver Lake—Page 50, Toppenish Natl. Wildlife Refuge—Page 108, McNary—Page 112, Umatilla Natl. Wildlife Refuge—Page 114.

AVOCETS

Gloyd Seeps W.R.A.—Page 90, Upper Potholes—Page 94.

SANDHILL CRANES

Ridgefield Natl. Wildlife Refuge and nearby areas—Page 48, Columbia Natl. Wildlife Refuge and nearby areas—Page 98, State Highway 108 near Mansfield (contact Washington State Game Department, Regional Office, Ephrata).

BALD EAGLES

San Juan Islands—Page 12, Olympic Natl. Park Ocean Strip—Page 36, Marblemount Eagle Sanctuary—Page 54.

CURLEWS

Occasionally on the farm fields of Eastern Washington.

A bighorn sheep caught unaware near Loomis

MOUNTAIN BLUEBIRDS

Colockum W.R.A.—Page 68, Oak Creek W.R.A.—Page 72, Mt. Rainier Natl. Park—Page 76.

SEALS

Dungeness Natl. Wildlife Refuge—Page 26, Olympic Natl. Park—Page 30, Washington Islands Natl. Wildlife Refuge—Page 34.

1 San Juan Islands
San Juan Islands National Wildlife Refuge and San Juan Islands National Historic Park

Best season: Anytime
Highlights: Seabirds, eagles
Camping: On major islands, marine parks
Contact: Refuge Mgr., Nisqually Natl. Wildlife Refuge, P.O. Box 1756, Olympia. 206-753-9467

The tips of drowned mountains, sculpted by waves and wind, make one of the world's most picturesque island chains here in the northwest corner of Washington. From barren rocks to big islands with farms, resorts, and fishing ports, the San Juans are host to a surprising variety of wildlife: birds of near-desert, ocean dwellers like seals, whales and sea lions; nesting bald eagles, pesty hordes of hares that the eagles feed on. Unfortunately, you need a boat to see some of what the islands have to offer. And some island wildlife should be stayed away from.

Take bicycle tours of the four big islands accessible by ferry. They make good day trips. There are parks and private campgrounds if you want to stay longer. As the San Juans are in the Olympic Mountains' "rain shadow," you have a fair chance of a dry outing even in winter.

On your trip, stop often for slow looks around with binoculars, especially in early morning and toward dusk. The islands have small populations of most Western Washington mammals. But some carnivores are missing. They may have been killed or trapped, or they may need a larger range and more prey than the islands provide. Some animals have changed slightly in island isolation: Mink on the San Juans tend to be larger and lighter than those on the mainland. River otter have adapted to life in salt water.

San Juan Island is particularly interesting, with its hordes of European hares gone wild, skylarks brought from Europe to Canada and flown from British Columbia, and a good chance of seeing a bald eagle or an osprey in a snag near the island's south tip. Look for birds of dry Eastern Washington, like the Vesper sparrow, in this rain-shadow area. (San Juan Island also has national recreation areas at English Camp and American Camp, remnants of the serio-comic "Pig War" here.)

If you have a boat you can visit nature preserves on Waldron and Cypress Islands; or the popular boaters' "parks" of Jones, Matia, and Turn Islands. Stay away, though, from the small rocky islets. Most of them are existing or proposed wild-

Bald eagle on San Juan Island

Gull Island, one of the small islands in the San Juans

life refuges where you might disturb nesting gulls, puffins, auklets, or other seabirds. A good rule of thumb is: If you can see what is going on with binoculars, you are too close.

But from a boat or even the ferry from Anacortes you can watch the wildlife in channels between Islands. There is something at every season, much of it comic. Sea birds sometimes gather in hovering and diving assemblies over schools of herring or in spots where the islands' complex tidal currents bring food to the surface. Squeaking Harlequin ducks in clown suits dive near rocks. Loons float so low they look as if they were about to sink. Chunky black Rinoceros auklets with yellow horns on their bills; Tufted puffins with bulbous red beaks and drooping ivory "locks" like drunken old men splash along the water to take off on their short wings. Dignified Western grebes look down their noses at it all.

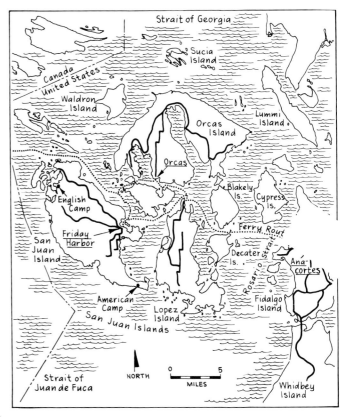

Wood duck house

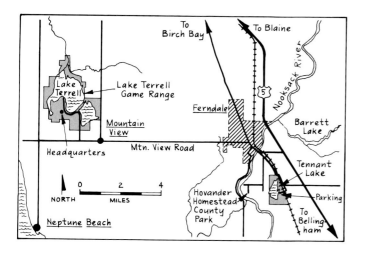

2 Lake Terrell Wildlife Recreation Area

Best season: Spring, summer
Highlights: Waterbirds
Camping: No
Contact: Wash. St. Game Dept., Regional Office, 1100 E. College Way, Mt. Vernon. 206-424-1177

Stop at Lake Terrell and its satellite, shallow Tennant Lake, in winter to see the usual assortment of Western Washington waterbirds, in summer to see unusual ones—comic loons and elegant Wood ducks.

To get to this northernmost of Western Washington W.R.A.s, take the Ferndale exit from Interstate Highway 5, eight miles north of Bellingham. From Ferndale, go east on Mountain View Road. Turn right at the blinking light onto Lake Terrell Road to get to Lake Terrell and W.R.A. headquarters.

Following the railroad tracks south from Ferndale will get you to Tennant Lake. But no signs mark the W.R.A. here and only a boardwalk edges the shallow, waterlily-choked lake. The Game Department so far has bought only the east side of the lake. It hopes to acquire the rest soon, and join the W.R.A. to Hovander Homestead County Park, a charming spot where families with children can enjoy an old farm house, antique farm implements, and barnyard animals.

These are places for day visits: Camping is not allowed in the W.R.A.s or in the county park. Late spring through summer probably is the best time for a visit. Walking is easier then than in the swamped winter. And the marshy lake with plenty of cover is a favorite bird-nesting area.

If you watch quietly, you can see the downy golden ducklings led by mother Mallards and by shyer, smaller teal. By putting up nest boxes, W.R.A. managers also have drawn a fair-sized population of Wood ducks, the elegant birds whose irridescent plumage and drooping green crests almost led to their extinction. They were sought as trout-fly material as well as for flesh.

The nest boxes also have drawn a few Hooded mergansers, another uncommon and exotic-looking duck that, like the Wood duck, rears its young in old woodpecker holes. These little divers with their fan-shaped black-and-white headdresses, and narrow "sawbills" used to grasp fish, seem to flee civilization: Their numbers in Washington have fallen.

This northern lowland lake also has kept another bird that fled as civilization took over in the rest of Western Washington: the Common loon. In black and white summer plumage like a neat collar and checked coat, the loons laugh, howl, and coo through the summer. Families seem to "play" together: They splash about, laughing and literally running on the water as if footracing.

While you are there, enjoy some common but still comic birds of lowland Washington waters: Homely gray pied-billed grebes wearing their black neck-ties of courtship, and giving a love-call between a laugh and a groan; or later, dogged by their constantly complaining convict-striped young. Watch, too, the squabbling of American coots, the familiar charcoal birds with white bills and absurdly big chartreuse legs and feet.

Hovander homestead farm

Trumpeter swans on Barney Lake

3 Trumpeter Lakes
Barney, Clear and Beaver Lakes

Best season: Fall—spring
Camping: No
Contact: Wash. St. Game Dept., Regional Office, 1100 E. College Way, Mt. Vernon. 206-424-1177

Barney, Clear, and Beaver Lakes are three rather ordinary Western Washington lakes where you can see something extraordinary: Washington's largest wintering group of Trumpeter swans, North America's largest waterbird and a rare and endangered species.

The unprepossessing lakes, edged by farms, suburbs, and brushy young woods, are just east of Mt. Vernon about 60 miles north of Seattle. From Interstate Highway 5, take exit 227, the College Way exit, just north of Mt. Vernon and go east on College Way (State Highway 538). Turn left on Martin Road just past the junior college. From the high shoulder just before Martin Road curves left, look down at the lake to the right. (This is one place where a birdwatcher's telescope is a real advantage.)

If the swans are not there, continue around the lake to the north on La Venture, Francis, and Swan Roads. Check for swans in the fields as you cross Nookachamps Creek. Continue to the resort town of Clear Lake, and look for swans from the public fishing accesses to Clear and Beaver Lakes. Take Old Day Creek Road just north of town and drive .4 miles east to reach the Clear Lake access. For Beaver Lake, turn southeast on the unsigned Beaver Lake Road just south of the 76 Station at the south edge of town. Signs saying "Public Fishing" mark both access points.

You can look for the Trumpeters any time from October through March. (After hunting season is best.) There is no camping or hiking here—The lakes are not even public property. But this is a "must" stop on a wildlife trip to the Skagit Flats for Snow geese or to Marblemount for eagles.

The big, long-necked birds with white plumage set off by black bills and feet have an elegant and aristocratic look as they glide on the water. They spoil it a bit when they tip sterns in air to stretch their long necks underwater for food; or "sunbathe" with one foot waggling in the air, a habit of many waterbirds. They have a different, wilder kind of beauty when they fly—in lines with long necks extended, moving on powerful, slow wingbeats with the storm wind in their voices.

Trumpeter swans

These swans, whose range once spanned Central and Western North America, probably became rare for a number of reasons: Big and fairly incautious, they made easy targets. They nested where farms and settlement took over the marshy prairie lakes where they built their nests, huge platforms of vegetation up to five feet across. (The Whistling swan, still fairly common, nests on Arctic tundra.) Trumpeters lay few eggs for a waterbird, and so did not rebuild quickly.

Now strictly protected, the Trumpeters seem to be making a small comeback. A small transplanted group nests at Turnbull National Wildlife Refuge near Spokane, and handfuls of wintering Trumpeters are turning up here and there in Washington.

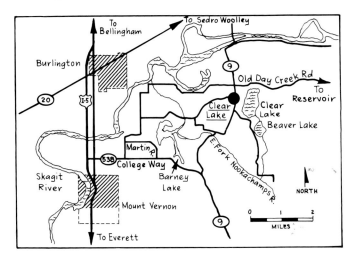

4 Skagit
Wildlife Recreation Area

Best season: Fall—spring
Highlights: Snowgeese, waterbirds, hawks
Camping: No
Contact: Wash. St. Game Dept., Regional Office, 1100 E. College Way, Mt. Vernon 206-424-1177

Air view of the Skagit Flats

A cloud of Snow geese cry in the wind as winter sun slants low across gray and gold flats, broken by gnarled gray drift stumps and rocky hillocks. It is easy to see why this area is a magnet for Washington artists as well as for wildlife watchers.

This big W.R.A.—almost 10,000 areas—stretches for miles along the Puget Sound shore, where the Skagit and Stillaguamish Rivers leave their fertile flood plains and wander to salt water through sloughs and across broad tide flats. You can reach several pleasant walks and watching points from Conway, just west of Exit 221 from the Interstate 5 freeway, 50 miles north of Seattle.

From Fir Island Road heading west from Conway, a left onto Mann Road takes you to W.R.A. headquarters and an easy loop walk of about two miles on dikes, where you have a good chance of seeing most of the W.R.A.'s wildlife types. Maupin Road, which continues west where Fir Island Road turns north, takes you to Jensen Access with a magnificent view of the tideflats. (It also is a popular clam-digging spot.) At the end of Rawlins Road, turning west from Fir Island Road about a mile further north, there is poor parking, but a short walk takes you to the North Fork of the Skagit and perhaps the W.R.A.'s most beautiful scenery.

While you drive, keep a lookout for swans, geese and ducks in farmers' fields outside the W.R.A. You can continue on Fir Island Road across the Skagit, take a right on Beaver Marsh Road, and look for Whistling swans grazing like sheep in their favorite fields, in the loop of Beaver Marsh, Calhoun, and Bradshaw Roads.

About 2½ miles south of Conway on the Stanwood-Conway Road, a W.R.A. sign points you to Milltown Island, a pleasant walk in fields and woods. Just west of the bridge over the Stillaguamish outside Stanwood, you can go south on Smith Road to an old farm facing Port Susan, and take another field-and-dike walk with views of the flats there.

The Skagit W.R.A. does not allow camping. Pick a high or incoming tide or a windy day for a visit, or the birds may be so far out on the flats that you need a boat or a duck-hunter's waders to see them. Any time of year is good for a visit, but winter may be most interesting and distinctive.

This area may be Northwest Washington's single most important area for waterbirds. Spring and fall bring resting shorebirds, gulls, terns, ducks, and geese. Winter is the most likely time to see eagles and other hawks. Washington's only large wintering population of Brant are nearby on Padilla Bay. (Look for them from waterside roads.) In the Skagit area are Whistling swans and, most famous, the Snow geese. The birds that winter here are a distinctive population that breeds only on Wrangell Island, 90 miles north of Siberia. When spring comes late to the ice-locked island, eggs and young may die and the flock dwindles. But 25,000 to 30,000 geese are normal here. Look for them on the flats, in farmers' fields—or simply listen for their voices. When they fly you can hear their high cries more than a mile away.

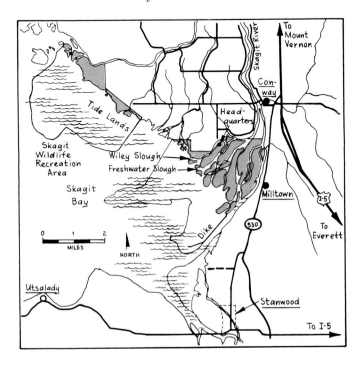

Snow geese

Red-tailed hawk (Harlan's hawk)

5 Stillwater
Wildlife Recreation Area

Best season: Winter, spring
Highlights: Songbirds, beaver and other small mammals
Camping: Undeveloped
Contact: Wash. St. Game Dept., Regional Office, 509 Fairview Ave. N., Seattle. 206-464-7764

Fields, alder woods, ponds, and sloughs in a river's floodplain make up this four-part W.R.A. on the Snohomish and its tributary, the Snoqualmie. These are not spectacular spots, or places where you are especially likely to see rare or distinctive animals. The Ebey Island segment can be reached only by boat. But the upriver three make part of a nice outing: Explore the green dairying valley of the Snoqualmie from Snoqualmie Falls (near the town of Snoqualmie) on down. Stop at the W.R.A.s to stretch your legs in an easy stroll. Enjoy the busy world of ordinary field and riverside wildlife of lowland Western Washington.

The W.R.A.'s Stillwater segment is 2½ miles north of Carnation on the Carnation-Duvall Road. Signs saying "public hunting" direct you into two parking lots. From there you can walk on service roads through corn fields (about a fifth of the crop is left for wildlife) and along Harris Creek, ponds, sloughs, and the river itself.

The Cherry Valley segment is fields and alder woods along a creek northeast of Duvall. Take the Cherry Hill Road just north of town. At about a mile, park in the signed area beside a big white barn and walk across the road and into the W.R.A.

Two Rivers segment, fields and a walk along a wooded oxbow lake that was once a river channel, is 5½ miles north of Duvall. Turn left on 203rd N.E. where the sign says State Dairy Farm. Pass the prison honor farm, go left on Hi-Bridge Road, and park in the signed lot before you reach the bridge. (For the rest of your valley tour, cross the bridge and loop back to Carnation on the West Snoqualmie Valley and Carnation Farm Roads.)

Camping is allowed. But there are no really pretty spots for it and the only facilities are outhouses in the parking lots. The day trip is interesting anytime. But hunters keep the W.R.A.s busy and noisy in hunting season. At Stillwater and Cherry Valley you may also find hunters training dogs any time of year.

This is a good place to look for the many signs of beaver, for muskrat houses and the "baby's hand" tracks of raccoons. The animals themselves are active mostly at night. With luck, you might spot an otter, a mink, or an osprey—all wild fishers in the valley. Kingfishers rattle and plummet from water-

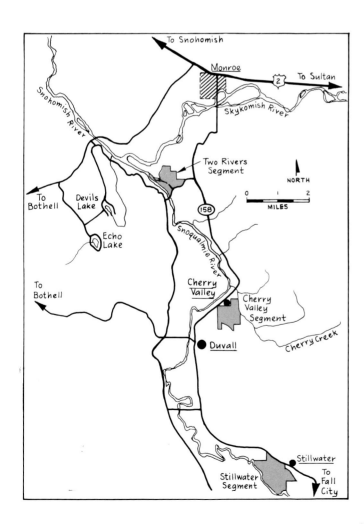

Harris Creek

side limbs. Great blue herons stalk in ponds and flooded fields.

In winter, you will startle flocks of hundreds of Mallards and whistling Wigeons from the fields. The less-common ducks are here, too. You may see an eagle, or Whistling swans.

White clouds of gulls gather in the stubble. In early spring they are joined by black clouds of handsome male Red-winged blackbirds, adding their ringing calls to the gulls' screams and the crows' raucous caws. When the dull brown Red-wing females arrive later, the polygamous males court them absurdly, bowing almost upside-down to show off their red chevrons.

April and May bring a full complement of five kinds of coursing, darting swallows. Quail and pheasant crow in courtship. There are flycatchers and bright songbirds: warblers, red-and-yellow tanagers, goldfinches in black and yellow summer plumage.

Medicine Creek Treaty Tree

6 Nisqually Delta
Nisqually National Wildlife Refuge and Nisqually Wildlife Recreation Area

Best season: Spring, summer, winter
Highlights: Waterbirds, shorebirds, raptors; canoeing
Camping: No
Contact: Refuge Mgr., Nisqually Natl. Wildlife Refuge, P.O. Box 1756, Olympia. 206-753-9467

This peaceful river delta just off busy Interstate Highway 5, containing both a state W.R.A. and a national wildlife refuge, is a sort of top-flight all-round "birding" spot, where a variety of habitats gives many creatures what they want. Besides birds, the area offers a beautiful view of Sound and islands, pleasant canoeing, and interesting history: The British Hudson's Bay Co. established a trading post just upriver in 1833. McAllister Creek was formerly Medicine Creek, and just north of the freeway you can walk past the "Treaty Tree," the spot where the Medicine Creek treaties were signed—leading to the Indian wars of the 1850s and the Indian-fishing-rights disputes of today.

To get there, take the Nisqually exit from Interstate Highway 5 between Tacoma and Olympia. Parking near the refuge entrance is poor. It probably is best to park near the restaurants and service stations south of the freeway, and walk north under the freeway to the dike. The dike is broken as this is written, and the refuge, normally split into fresh and salt-water marshes, is flooded with salt water. When it is repaired there probably will be an easy loop dike walk around the federal refuge and to much of the state land. (Crossing the federal area is banned, to avoid disturbing the birds.)

You also can walk along McAllister Creek, or make it a canoe trip: Take Martin Way south from the filling station-restaurant area, cross the freeway on Meridian Road, and follow the signs to the boat launch at Luhr Access on Nisqually Head. As tides reach well upstream, check a tide table so that you will not be paddling against a strong ebb or flood.

Nisqually's birds are likely to be scattered, skittish, and well offshore during hunting season. But the area is a good place to visit any other time of year. Camping is not allowed. But if you live in one of the nearby cities, this is a good place to go many times, to watch how an area's wildlife changes with the seasons, and how different kinds of animals use its salt marsh, fresh water marsh, trees, brush, and fields.

Nisqually's yearly cycle is typical of the region. Spring and summer nesting of songbirds, swallows, quail, Killdeer, and waterbirds—Mallards, teal, Pied-billed grebes—are followed, in early fall, by hordes of migrating gulls, terns, sandpipers and other shorebirds, and dabbling ducks. Divers arrive later. Wintering ducks—mostly Wigeon, Pintails, teal, and Mallards—and wintering shorebirds, mostly Dunlin, are joined by hawks—mostly Marsh and Red-tailed. Spring brings the migrants again, moving faster than in fall but often in brighter plumage, and going through interesting courtship rituals. Anytime, there are those interesting birds built for their tasks: Belted kingfishers shaped like plummets, with big heads and small feet; and elongated Great blue herons, wading on stilt legs and using their long neck and bill like a spear.

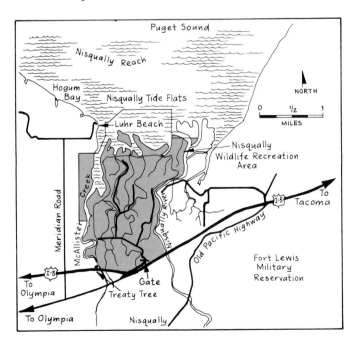

23

Scatter Creek barn

Camas

Columbine

7 Scatter Creek
Wildlife Recreation Area

Best season: Spring
**Highlights: Songbirds, small mammals, wild-
flowers**
Camping: No
**Contact: Wash. St. Game Dept., Regional Of-
fice, 905 E. Heron. 206-532-9680**

Scatter Creek is nothing spectacular. Its fields,
woods, and a creek and beaver pond on the prairie
country between Olympia and Centralia offer you a
quiet place to take a walk, and a wild community
with a distinctive character of its own.

To reach this W.R.A., take the Maytown-Little-
rock exit from Interstate Highway 5 six miles south
of Olympia. Turn south on Case Road just west of
the freeway. Six miles south, a small W.R.A. sign
and a red barn tell you you have reached the Case
segment of the area. To reach the Township segment and W.R.A. headquarters, continue about
another mile to Township Road, (also called 183rd
Ave. S.W.) turn west on Township and then north
on Guava. (You also can reach Township or 183rd
by driving north from exit 88 on the freeway.)

This is a place for a few hours of strolling only.
The service roads are closed to vehicles. Neither
segment has camping facilities. Spring probably is
the best time for a visit, when birds are singing and
nesting and the wildflowers of the prairies are in
bloom. Hunters training dogs can be a distraction
in the Case segment, open for dog training year-
round. But Township is closed to the trainers April
through July.

The prairies and oak bottomlands of this region
are a unique bit of wild Washington with an interesting natural and human history. Ice Age glaciers coming down from Canada reached south only
to about Tenino, a few miles to the north. Gravel
washed from the ice sheet's "toe" made the well-
drained prairies. The low rainfall around Centralia and Chehalis also led to a plant and animal
community unlike others in wet Western
Washington.

Oak groves shelter the Western gray squirrel, the
big shy tree squirrel found in Washington only in
the oak and pine communities scattered from here
around the south and southeast edges of the Cascades. The prairies also harbor the Mazama pocket
gopher, a close kin of Eastern Washington's
Northern pocket gopher. These burrowers are
found in Western Washington only on these gla-
cial-outwash prairies and in the high Olympics.

You will find other life at Scatter Creek reminis-
cent of dry, open Eastern Washington: songbirds

like the Horned lark, flowers of blue camas, its
bulbs once harvested by Indians in spring
gatherings here like great camas-harvesting
gatherings in Eastern Washington.

The low, open country also was an Indian and
settlers' trail from the lower Columbia to Puget
Sound. (Interstate 5 continues this function.)
White settlers made some of their first tries at
farming on these open prairies, but soon found wetter wooded land better despite the work of clearing.

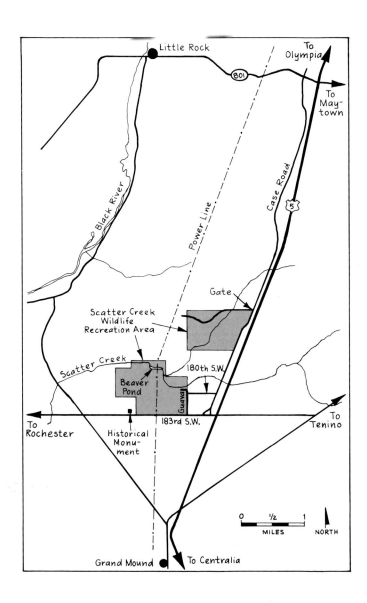

25

8 Dungeness National Wildlife Refuge

Best season: Winter, spring
Highlights: Waterbirds, shorebirds, seals; canoeing, beach hike
Camping: Adjacent recreation area
Contact: Refuge Mgr., Nisqually Natl. Wildlife Refuge, P.O. Box 1756, Olympia. 206-753-9467

Dungeness Spit is the place to go when you are hit with a midwinter longing for driftwood, sand, and salt water. The 5½-mile-long sandspit in the rain shadow of the Olympic Mountains often is sunny when the rest of Western Washington is dreary gray. In September, and from the end of hunting season through May, it offers you a look at thousands of ducks, geese, shorebirds, terns—and the likelihood that a playful-looking spotted Harbor seal will come and take a look at you.

The fishhook-shaped spit sheltering a shallow bay is on the north shore of the Olympic Peninsula, between Sequim and Port Angeles. From State Highway 101, turn north on Kitchin Road 4.3 miles west of Sequim and follow the signs 3.5 miles to Dungeness Recreation Area. A well-marked trail takes you from this camping and picnic area to the beach. On the way, you pass meadows edging the high bluff overlooking the Strait of Juan de Fuca, and bits of spruce forest where you are scolded by chipmunks and chickadees.

The long walk out the spit in sand is tiring, but worth it. Be sure you take drinking water.

At the flats at the base of the spit in migration times, look for Whimbrels and plovers, yellowlegs and dowitchers, Sanderlings and other delicate, probing shorebirds. Out on the bay, roughly from October to May, rafts of dignified Western grebes glare scornfully from their red eyes. (The red eyes of seabirds are believed to be a protection against glare from the water.) Well north along the spit, where there are beds of eelgrass offshore, look for flocks of Brant, the little black sea geese with white collars. They nod and cackle at each other, maintaining the flock's rank order and their own sense of personal space.

Well out on the spit also is the best place to see surface-feeding or "dabbling" ducks—including the Wigeons that steal from diving birds.

The spit is one of the nicest places to watch Surf and White-winged scoters, the comic ducks of salt water. They are definite ugly ducklings: heavy-bodied, short-necked, with bumpy orange bills and white clown markings on their faces. They play fol-

low-the-leader: If one dives, all dive. They swim and fly in lines. After a spell of diving, all rest and preen a bit. Then it is time for a game of tag, with one after another duck as "it." (Actually, the game is courtship, with the dull brown females as leaders and, in the long run, prizes.)

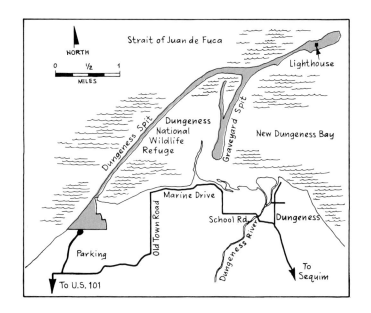

Canada goose nest

8 Dungeness National Wildlife Refuge

Dungeness Lighthouse and Mount Baker

Harbor seals

Sea gulls

9 Olympic National Park

Best season: Anytime
Highlights: Mountain goats, elk; back-
     packing, climbing, rain forest,
     beach hike
Camping: Yes
Contact: Park Supt., Olympic Natl. Park, 600
     E. Park Ave., Port Angeles, 98362.
     206-452-9235

Deer on Hurricane Ridge

From glaciers through rain forest down to rocky ocean coast, magnificent Olympic National Park offers the wildlife watcher far more than this guide can even touch on.

Oddly enough, one of the highlights of a hike through the park's highlands is not even native to the area. Mountain goats are native to the Cascades, but not to the Olympics. They have spread through the range since they were introduced about 50 years ago. Perhaps because they have never been hunted, they often seem as curious about hikers as hikers are about them. Many an Olympic wanderer has tales of his close-up encounter with the stocky, white-bearded "king of the mountain," who watches him curiously or defiantly, then tosses his head and picks his way calmly off up some impossible crag.

The most likely spots for such meetings are around Lake Constance and Mt. Gladys; and, probably best of all, on the side of Mt. Angeles.

In the park's rocky, flowery highlands fat, grizzled-to-yellowish Olympic marmots will sit up and whistle as you approach their burrow colonies. A little smaller and browner than his Cascades cousin, the Hoary marmot, and with coat often calico-patched yellow and brown, the Olympic marmot is a separate type that has evolved over centuries of isolation in the peaks.

Wildflowers found nowhere else in the world, too, have developed or survived in this range that stands far from other mountains. Best known of these flowers is the Piper's harebell (Campanula piperii). The tiny alpine plant is almost hidden by the nodding blue-purple bells of bloom.

Lower in the mountains, don't be surprised if you find a Black bear sharing your trail or feeding in some lush meadow. Douglas squirrels trill at you from the evergreens.

Deer abound. But far better known are the native Roosevelt elk, that survived in the wilderness here when they were almost wiped out in the Cascades. This coastal type is far larger than the Rocky Mountain elk native farther east, and transplanted to the Cascades. But Roosevelt elk have been less coveted by trophy hunters because their antlers are shorter. Some of the elk wander from

subalpine heights in summer to ocean coast in winter. Even if you do not see them, you may see their effects. In the Hoh River Valley, for example, they keep a park-like trim on grass and brush, adding to the beauty of this rain-forest area.

The park's wilderness beaches offer you migrant birds of shoreline areas, rare glimpses of the birds of open ocean—like flocks of shearwaters skimming the waves on fall migration—and perhaps a peek into the colonial family life of birds breeding on the refuge rocks offshore. (See Washington Islands National Wildlife Refuge.)

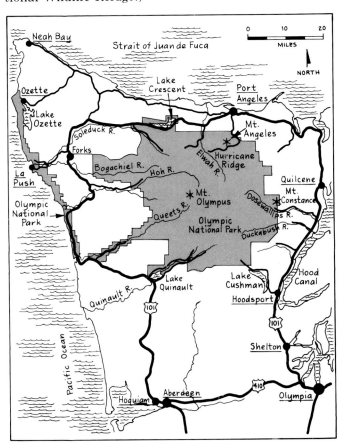

Elk crossing the Hoh River

31

Deer near Toleak Point

Mountain goat on side of Mount Angeles

9 Olympic National Park

Skunk near Toleak Point

Olympic marmot

Piper bellflower

Salmon in Soleduck River

Harbor seals

10 Washington Islands National Wildlife Refuge

Best season: May, June
Highlights: Nesting seabirds
Camping: In Olympic Natl. Park
Contact: Refuge Mgr., Willapa Natl. Wildlife
Refuge, Ilwaco, 98624. 206-484-3482

For eons, the surf-battered reefs and pinnacles scattered along more than 100 miles of Washington's northern ocean coast have been a refuge where seabirds raised their young. Government merely underlined nature's decree, making it illegal as well as dangerous to land on these 870-odd rocky islets, some with tiny wind-sculpted forests and miniature meadows.

From the shore, though, you can get tantalizing glimpses of birds' not-so-private love lives in these close-packed colonies. (This is one place where distance generally demands a birdwatcher's telescope.)

The best time for a visit to watch seabirds probably is May through early July, the islet nesting season. It is also arrival time for male Harlequin ducks, as they come down from their mountain breeding spots to go through their flightless molt in the safety of the rocks. Much of the beach is Indian reservation—Respect their closures. You can camp and hike in the part that is Olympic National Park.

The Coast Guard station at Pt. Grenville probably gives you the closest look at the nesting colonies. But the station now allows visitors only from 1 to 3 p.m. weekdays or 1 to 4 weekends, and a coastguardsman must accompany you to the cliffs. Spots that require only short hikes are Kalaloch and nearby Ruby Beach; Rialto Beach and Second Beach near La Push; and Cape Flattery near Neah Bay. Or you can take tougher hikes of two to three miles from Lake Ozette to Sand Point or Cape Alava. (You can rent a boat at La Push or Neah Bay and go out in calm weather, but stay away from the islets for the birds' sake and your own safety.)

The rocky coast offers some of the most graceful of birds—petrels flitting gracefully at dusk, shearwaters skimming the waves on migration. It also offers some of the oddest-looking: Sleek and rather snake-like cormorants and Common murres, the murres warming a single egg laid on bare rock. Or the Tufted puffins, chunky black birds with red beaks, white faces, and yellowish ear-tufts; pairs digging burrows in the thin soil to lay their single egg.

Shapes like these are adapted to a life of diving in open water, and this is the reason the birds need their island havens guarded by cliffs and sea. They can no longer move well on land. Some must launch themselves from cliffs or patter a long way on open water before their short wings carry them aloft.

Keep an eye out for a lucky glimpse of marine mammals: Harbor seals, Northern sea lions, whales, dolphins, even the recently re-introduced Sea otter. Onshore, expect the unexpected-looking shorebirds of rocky beaches, like the Black oystercatcher with orange, chisel-shaped bill.

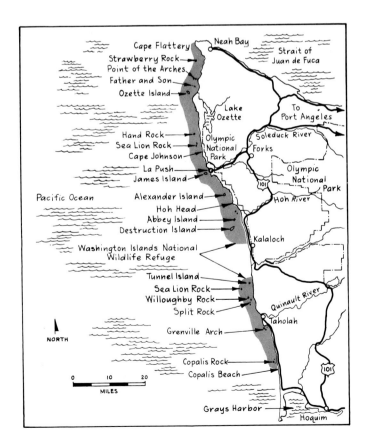

Air view of refuge islets south of Third Beach

Abandoned railroad trestle

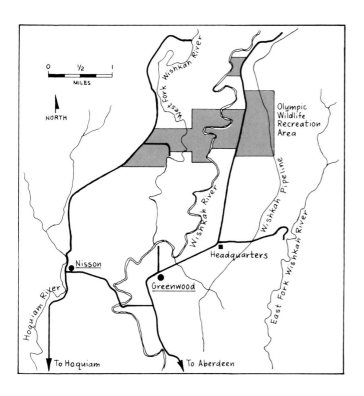

11 Olympic Wildlife Recreation Area

Best season: Anytime
Highlights: Elk, deer, small mammals, song-
             birds
Camping: Undeveloped
Contact: Wash. St. Game Dept., Regional Of-
          fice, 905 E. Heron, Aberdeen. 206-532-
          9680

This 1,500-acre W.R.A. in the southern foothills of the Olympics is just scattered bits of fields and brush amid commercial tree farms. But it is a fascinating winter range for elk and deer; and a spot to enjoy fishing, canoeing, mushroom hunting, and the lowland wildlife of Western Washington.

The Game Department ownerships lie in the valleys of the Wishkah and Upper Wynoochee Rivers. Fortunately, they are scattered among logging lands that are also mostly open to the public. Take B Street north from Aberdeen: It becomes Wishkah Road, running up the west side of the river, and about 13 miles from Aberdeen and a half mile past the town of Greenwood you reach W.R.A. headquarters. Staying on the road will take you through several pieces of state land. Small dirt roads lead left to undeveloped camping spots near the river. There are no developed camping facilities.

In this rainy part of Washington, spring through fall give you the best chance of a dry visit. But winter is the best time to see the elk and deer. Estimates are that about 1,800 deer and 3,200 elk from 120 square miles use the area at various times in winter.

The W.R.A.'s history is a fascinating tale of how man has changed wildlife and what he must now do to cope with it.

The old evergreen forests that once covered the area were cut between the 1890s and the 1930s. You can still see the remains of old logging-railroad trestles and "splash dams" used to send logs downstream on a rush of water—with devastating effects on salmon and trout and their spawning areas.

Old-timers say deer and elk were rare in the area until at least the 1930s, after the land had been cleared and was growing up again, and logging had moved higher. Then, growing numbers of deer and elk coming down from the mountains in winter began to invade farms, damaging orchards, crops, and fences. Although the Game Department made its buys in the 1950s to cut down the damage, many

Wishkah River

old-time settlers opposed the "land grab"—a rather common local reaction to new wildlife areas.

Meticulous care goes into wooing the elk and deer onto this range. Elk were watched carefully one winter to see just what kind of green they would paw through snow for, and just this mixture of grasses and clover is planted. A particular type of oats that draws elk in early fall is planted. Fertilizing is timed to make plants grow just when the elk get hungry. Logging is carried on so as to make small clearings with cover for the animals in between.

Of course, there is more here to enjoy than elk and deer. Band-tailed pigeons coo and puff their chests, Ruffed grouse strut and drum in the woods in spring. Look for Snowshoe hares at the edges of brush near dusk; for tracks of night-moving raccoon and skunks; and for signs of beaver.

Sea gulls

Wreck of the Catala

12 Oyhut
Wildlife Recreation Area

Best season: Winter, spring, early fall
Highlights: Shorebirds, waterbirds
Camping: No
Contact: Wash. St. Game Dept., Regional Office, 905 E. Heron, Aberdeen. 206-532-9680

Next time you go to Ocean Shores, leave the pounding Pacific surf for a quiet walk on the sheltered bay side, in this 682-acre state game area near the resort peninsula's sandy southern tip. It is a birdwatcher's small paradise: Sandy beach, salt meadow and brush, driftwood, ponds, and a rock jetty draw an amazing variety of birds passing along the great migration highway of the coast. The W.R.A. is one of the state's likelier places for spotting rare species.

To get there, drive to the motel city of Ocean Shores, about 27 miles west of Aberdeen. Turn off of State Highway 115 into the big Ocean Shores gates. Then turn right almost immediately onto Ocean Shores Blvd. South about four miles, you can turn east onto Marine View Drive and park in the lot with the sign explaining the nearby wreck of the steamship Catala. Or continue south on Ocean Shores Blvd. to the peninsula tip, follow the loop east about half a mile, and park by the sewage treatment plant.

From either parking lot you can walk the half-ruined jetty and driftwood reef that separate Oyhut's saltwater sink from the bay. You also can skirt the W.R.A.'s west edge by auto.

Migration may bring more than eight kinds of gull, along with terns and the jaegers that rob them and the smaller gulls in acrobatic aerial chases. Least sandpipers, alarmed by a Marsh hawk, wheel and turn in perfect unison, so that the tight flock look now white, now brown. The shorebirds you see may include the American golden plover, whose migration from the Arctic to Argentina makes it long-distance champion among migrants. Look, too, for the oddly named Wandering tattler on the rock jetty; for whimbrels, willets, and knots. (These shorebird names are supposed to resemble their calls.)

The late winter, when the resort is almost deserted, has its own leisurely charm. Migration crowds are gone, too: Wildlife is less but you have it and the beach almost to yourself. Dignified Western grebes glide and clown-faced scoters play tag off the beach. A Red-throated loon looks silly as his name, floating low in the water and stretching his head up as if to see as he sinks. A Black turnstone actually does turn shells and bits of driftwood in his search for food on the jetty. Flocks of Pintails dabble, sleep, and bathe in the shallow sink inland.

Sand patterns

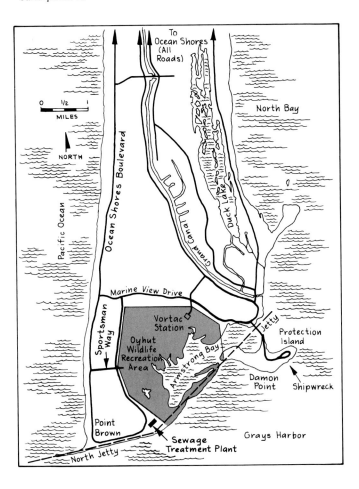

39

John's River

13 Johns River Wildlife Recreation Area

Best season: Winter, spring
Highlights: Hawks, marsh birds, waterfowl; canoeing
Camping: Undeveloped
Contact: Wash. St. Game Dept., Regional Office, 905 E. Heron, Aberdeen. 206-532-9680

Johns River and its two satellites, Palix River and Smith Creek, let you sample the peaceful, watery world that edges Southwest Washington's two big bays, Grays Harbor and Willapa. Decaying pilings, gnarled orchards, and lush abandoned pastures edge rivers' tidal mouths with their swamps and sloughs.

Johns River W.R.A., 1,229 acres, is the largest of the three, and the most varied and interesting. It includes woods and abandoned fields on both sides of the river, and a tidal swamp beyond the river mouth, accessible only by boat. Just across the highway from the W.R.A. are two of the distinctive industries of this corner of Washington: a small oyster-shucking operation and the big Ocean Spray plant that packs cranberries grown on the sandy, swampy soil here.

Drive south from Aberdeen 11 miles on State Highway 105. Unmarked gravel roads just north of the Johns River Bridge lead east into the W.R.A. But the best access is to turn east onto County Road 1740 just south of the bridge, and then turn left or north almost immediately onto an un-marked gravel road. This takes you to W.R.A. headquarters, a boat-launch ramp that was the old landing for the river ferry, and an easy walk of about a mile on the dike running upriver from the parking lot. (You can reach a similar dike walk from the unnamed gravel road that leads into the W.R.A. just north of the Ocean Spray plant on the other side of the river.)

The two satellites, 600-acre Smith Creek and 240-acre Palix River, lie on similar estuaries on Willapa Bay. Highway 105 cuts through the Smith Creek W.R.A., about ten miles west of Raymond. There is a boat launch ramp and parking lot. To reach Palix W.R.A., drive south from Raymond on State Highway 101. At .7 miles south of the boat launch on the Palix River, turn east or left, then left again a mile further on at the bottom of a hill. A half mile further on, a road turns left a short distance to the Game Department parking lot and another dike walk.

Unless you have a small boat, these dike walks probably are the best way to get the flavor of these areas. Camping is allowed but there are no developed spots for it.

Startled ducks

Anytime except hunting season is a good time for a visit, although winter is rainy and summer sometimes heavy with mosquitos. You may see deer or elk here at dusky hours. Expect Great blue herons flapping slowly along sloughs. Marsh hawks glide and wobble low over the fields, hunting unwary mice. These hawks' white rumps and this characteristic flight, with wings a bit above horizontal, make them easy to identify. Small birds skitter away, chirping in alarm. You, too, cause a disturbance: A marsh wren scolds you from the reeds; male Red-winged blackbrids scream about your head in nesting season. Ducks start and splash away.

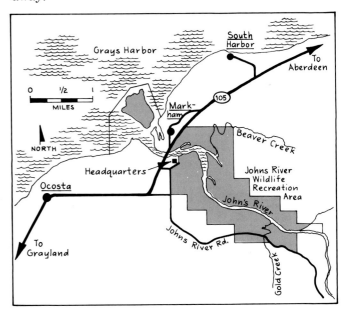

14 Willapa
National Wildlife Refuge

Best season: Winter, spring, summer
Highlights: Shorebirds, waterbirds, boating to Long Island; beach hike to Ledbetter Point
Camping: On Long Island
Contact: Refuge Mgr., Willapa Natl. Wildlife Refuge, Ilwaco, 98624. 206-484-3482

This three-part wildlife refuge in Washington's little-known southwest corner—Long Island, Willapa, and Leadbetter Point—shows you the world of Willapa Bay's silver sloughs and tideflats, teeming with life—plus salt meadows alive with songbirds and a wooded island.

From the junction of State Highways 4 and 101, drive 4.5 miles southwest on 101 to reach the neat white refuge headquarters. Here you can get maps and information on all three areas. A pond has two blinds set up for bird photographers.

You also can launch a canoe or small boat here to cross the narrow channel to Long Island.(The tide runs out a half mile, so be sure you have a tide table and the refuge handout map to tell you when you can reach certain beaches.) The island is 5,000 acres of mossy woods (including a stand of virgin cedars) trimmed with meadows and salt marshes. You can picnic or camp at any one of seven campgrounds and hike miles of easy trails. Geese graze in the meadows, shorebirds use the flats, and the woods have songbirds, Blue grouse, and typical mammals including elk, deer and bear.

About 5.5 miles farther west on Highway 101, just after you cross the Bear River, a small refuge sign on Jeldness Road directs you 1.2 miles north to some of the best and easiest waterfowl-watching in Washington. A walk of less than a half mile on the gravel road past the Willapa refuge gate shows you hundreds of coots, scaups, Canvasbacks, Buffleheads, Mallards, Pintails, Shovelers, and other birds in this half-drowned maze of ponds and sloughs. (Early fall, late winter and spring are best.)

Five miles farther on, turn north at the blinking yellow light onto Peninsula Road, that takes you up the long outer edge of the bay past cattle, cranberry farms, woods, and picturesque oyster landings. A refuge sign on Yeaton Road points you two miles to grassy Willapa Refuge fields where you can see hundreds of Canada geese in fall, winter, and spring.

Continue north to Oysterville (about 16 miles from 101). The beautifully preserved little settlement was founded in 1854 to ship heaps of native

Great blue heron

oysters to San Francisco. Jog west about .2 miles, then north about 4.5 miles on Stackpole Road. You can park at the undeveloped state park and walk the beach from here, or continue roughly straight on a poor dirt road about a half mile to the refuge boundary where the woods break into dunes.

Hiking the bay side is best for wildlife watching. The ocean side has some characteristic birds, but you may have to share it with cars. (Crossing the marshy dunes and meadow between the two is difficult except in summer.) Fall and spring migrations are the best times, although the beach is beautiful any time of year—even winter, when the labyrinth of silver channels and dead gold grass is edged by a serpent of frozen foam. Pick a fairly high or incoming tide so the birds will be in sight.

Early spring through late April or early May brings flights of Brant, and White-fronted geese. There are gulls, terns, ducks, clouds of shorebirds.

Like other open spots along the mild coast, the meadow dunes are a winter refuge for birds that nest in alpine meadows and on Arctic tundra—Lapland longspurs, Horned larks, Water pipits, plovers, and occasional Snowy owls.

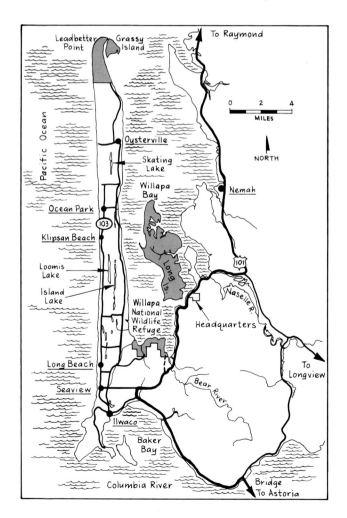

Whistling swans and Canada geese at headquarters pond

Sand verbena

Bear on Leadbetter Point

Sand dunes on Leadbetter Point

Turkey vulture

Gulls over the Columbia

Belted kingfisher

Columbian white-tailed deer and fawn. Collar and ear tag are part of a scientific study.

15 Columbian White-Tailed Deer National Wildlife Refuge

Best season: Any time
Highlights: Columbian white-tailed deer; boating to islands
Camping: Undeveloped, on White Island
Contact: Refuge Mgr., Rt. 1, Box 376C, Cathlamet, 98612. 206-795-4915

Come to this old farm and fishing country of the Lower Columbia to find a world that time forgot—and to discover the rich wildlife of the river bottom, including a rare subspecies of deer with a special place in history.

The 5,200-acre refuge lies between Cathlamet and Skamokawa, about 30 miles west of Interstate Highway 5 at Kelso. The drive on State Highway 4 takes you past dairy farms and deep woods, and past abandoned landings, old cannery piers and pilings that remind you of the busier days when steamboats plied the mighty river.

You can turn onto Steamboat Slough Road at Skamokawa and circle much of the refuge by car. The rough dirt road that crosses the refuge is often gated near the highway. You also can launch a small boat at the Cathlamet mooring basin or the boat-launch site near Skamokawa on Brooks Slough. By boat, you can reach Tenasilahee Island, a good place for a walk in pasture and woods; the thickly overgrown parts of Price and Hunting Islands that are in the refuge; and White Island, state owned and open to the public.

The deer swim the channels and live on the islands. But you are as likely to see them by driving the dike road that circles the refuge, or strolling in the fields to picnic in an alder grove.

The Lower Columbia stays green and rainy year-round. Any time of year is good for a visit. Try to be there in early morning or late afternoon, when the deer leave their daytime hiding places in thickets and come into the pastures to graze.

Circling the refuge on the dike road, you pass the beached hulk of a barge, leaning fences of rough wood. A snipe that has been probing the mud with absurdly long bill zig-zags away with a harsh "scape, scape." Red-tailed hawks, and perhaps a Bald eagle, watch and wait for prey. An otter waggles across the road and slides into the slough: mink, beaver, and otter, once plentiful throughout the river bottoms, find refuge here as do the deer. Whistling swans and other waterfowl are common from December through February.

The deer themselves usually will let you get quite close, especially if you stay in your car.

The Columbian white-tailed deer are a subspecies that once were common in lowland swamps and bottoms of Western Oregon and Washington as far north as Puget Sound. Lewis and Clark found

Columbia River at Skamokawa

them plentiful along the Columbia in 1806—they helped feed the explorers. But farming that eliminated the deer's browse and brush cover whittled their numbers. In the 1930s they were feared extinct.

This newest of Washington refuges, begun in 1972, seems to assure a safe home for at least a few hundred of the remaining Columbian white-tails.

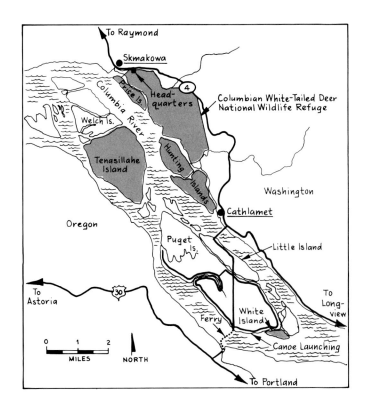

Red-tailed hawk

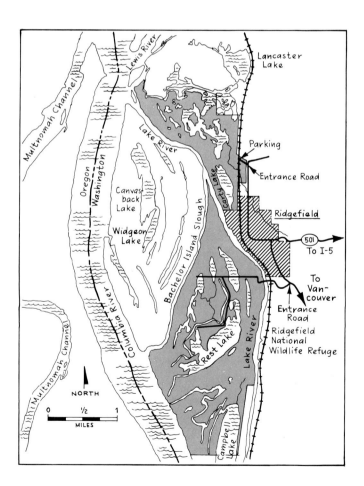

16 Ridgefield National Wildlife Refuge

Best season: Spring, summer
Highlights: Waterfowl, Sandhill cranes, songbirds; nature trail
Camping: No
Contact: Refuge Mgr., Ridgefield Natl. Wildlife Refuge, Box 467, Ridgefield, 98642. 206-695-3481

Pastures, groves and ponds on either side of the pretty little town of Ridgefield on the lower Columbia make a quiet resting place for man and wildlife. This is one of the few national wildlife refuges that welcomes you to its entire area (except during hunting season, when portions are closed).

To get there, take the Ridgefield exit from Interstate Highway 5, 15 miles north of Vancouver, and drive three miles west to the town. Or take Fruit Valley Road in Vancouver and follow the signs to Ridgefield. This route takes you past Vancouver Lake W.R.A. and near Shillapoo W.R.A.—a nice day-long wildlife tour.

In Ridgefield, pick up a refuge map and guide to the nature trail at North Third and Mill Street. The refuge has two parts. A half mile north of Ridgefield on Main Street, a refuge sign directs you into the Carty refuge unit. Park before you cross the railroad tracks, and walk from here. A faint jeep track with small wooden arrows, to your right just after you cross the entrance stile, is the Oak Grove Nature Trail, a mile walk. You can wander elsewhere in the groves of gnarled oaks, willow swamps, ponds, and pastures. But wear good boots in wet seasons.

The southern, River S unit is marked by a refuge sign on South Ninth Street (the road from Ridgefield to Vancouver) just south of town. This is the place to go when it is raining, and possibly the best for watching birds: It has about two miles of year-round gravel roads where you can watch from the warm, dry "blind" of your car.

As in most national wildlife refuges, camping is not permitted. There are outhouses at the parking lots, but no drinking water. Any time of year is good for a visit: The lush world along the Columbia is pleasant even in its frequent rains. Winter has its own charm with bare oaks and willows like witches' brooms, silvery water in golden stubble, and swans and great flocks of gray Canada geese on the refuge. Spring migration is "jumping" by March. It continues through April and May, with flowers added, and ducks, snipe, songbirds courting and nesting. Flickers and jays, fond of the oaks; Red-winged blackbirds and late-nesting goldfinches keep things from being too quiet in summer. Keep an eye peeled for the Scrub jay, a visitor to the state that ventures here from Oregon. Early fall brings blackberry picking and the return of early migrants. Non-hunters are barred on Wednesdays, weekends, and holidays during hunting season, but there is good watching on other days.

Year round, there are hunters here: Great blue herons stalking fish and frogs; Great horned owls that roost in deep groves by day and hunt rodents in the fields by night; and Red-tailed hawks, hunting these same mice by day.

The brown head you see swimming may not be the common muskrat, but a nutria—a South American animal brought by would-be fur farmers, gotten loose and become a pest.

A highlight is noisy flocks of hundreds of Sandhill cranes that make migration stopovers around early April and mid-October.

Pond in Ridgefield National Wildlife Refuge

Vancouver Lake

17 Vancouver Lake
Vancouver Lake and Shillapoo Wildlife Recreation Areas

Best season: Spring
Highlights: Waterfowl, raptors; boating to Caterpillar Is.
Camping: No
Contact: Wash. St. Game Dept., Vancouver Regional Office, 5405 N.E. Hazel Dell Ave., Vancouver, 98663. 206-696-6211

Take a Sunday drive or a picnic from Vancouver to visit these small state game areas: peaceful groves and pastures between the city's edge and the Columbia, in settings of dairy farms, filbert orchards, and fishing boats.

To reach them, start by driving west from the city center on West Fourth Plain Boulevard. Vancouver Lake W.R.A., 141 acres of fields and willow swamps along the south shore of Vancouver Lake, is reached by turning north onto Fruit Valley Road, then west a quarter of a mile further on onto gravel La Framboise Road. Look for pheasants and other small animals in the fields near the W.R.A. gate—Chukars and Chinese pheasants are released here for hunting in fall. You can drive along the lake front watching for ducks and geese in early fall and spring. But if the rafts of wildfowl are on another part of the 2,858-acre lake, you may see little besides black specks.

To get to Shillapoo, 276 acres in an area of croplands and wintertime ponds along the Columbia, stay on Fourth Plan to Lower River Road. It runs along Lake Vancouver and then becomes the road along the river dike. On one side are sloughs and fishing boats, on the other side farms and fields flooded to ponds, full of ducks, geese, herons, and Marsh hawks in winter. A state sign at the parking lot with outhouses marks the W.R.A., about eight miles from the city.

From the boat-launch ramp on the river side, you can launch a small boat to picnic on Caterpillar Island just opposite. It is leased by the state and has picnic tables. Or follow trails in the W.R.A.'s pastures and thickets.

If it is raining or you are just out for a drive, continue another three miles or so to the road's end. The views of birds in the winter-wet fields and seasonal lakes are better, and you can stay warm and dry in your car "blind" without frightening the flocks.

Both W.R.A.s are day-use areas, with no camping facilities. If they don't fill your day, head north 13 miles on Fruit Valley Road—the road to Ridgefield—and take in Ridgefield National Wildlife Refuge as well. Late winter and spring, from

Channel between mainland and Caterpillar Island

roughly January to May, probably is the most interesting time to see wildlife. Hawks and eagles are still down from the mountains. Canada geese and a few Whistling swans are moving north. Ducks, also on migration, are carrying on their noisy, chasing courtship rituals. Warblers, wrens, and other songbirds arrive and tune up. Several kinds of swallows dart over the water.

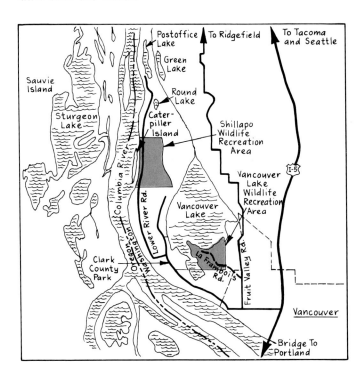

51

18 North Cascades National Park

Best season: Summer
Highlights: Backpacking, climbing, boat trips
Camping: Yes
**Contact: Park Supt., North Cascades Natl.
Park, 311 State St., Sedro Woolley.
206-855-1331**

Wildlife watching in this spectacularly rugged north end of the Cascade Range can be erratic. On one trip, the mountains seem to teem with mammals and birds. On the next, forests and high meadows seem empty. You are not likely to miss the wildlife, though. The scenery in North Cascades National Park, and adjacent Ross Lake and Lake Chelan National Recreation Areas, is too striking for that.

Even by comparison with other parts of the Cascades, the North Cascades' terrain can make it difficult to see animals. The glacier-gouged, knife-ridged mountains tend to go from ice and rock to dense woods, with relatively few open alpine and subalpine meadows and lakes between. You are unlikely to spot the Mountain goats that live in the rugged Picket Range. (They are a routine sight, though, on the winter boat ride up Lake Chelan on the way to Stehekin. Like many deer, they come low and graze on the steep lake shore.)

Deer sometimes nibble on greenery along the North Cascades Highway, or wander near campgrounds—as do Black bear. (Take the usual precautions with your food.)

In rock heaps and slides like those around Cascade Pass, you may see the Pika, the little short-eared relative of rabbits that survives at alpine heights. (His short ears and legs follow the rule that species in cold climates have short extremities, tending to preserve body heat.) Don't be surprised as an also-common Hoary marmot whistles at you in the same rock slide where Pikas squeal their "enk, enk." The two species often tunnel in the same rock piles. They eat similar foods, too. But they seem to avoid one out-competing the other because they have slightly different habits. Pikas, for example, cut "hay" and dry it in little haystacks. Marmots gorge themselves to get fat for a long winter sleep, which puts their peak harvest period at a slightly different time.

North Cascades mammal life can be as interesting for what you know but don't see as for what you do see. Big Beaver Valley is well named: Beaver, by keeping the valley floor ponded and swampy for centuries, have virtually governed the soil and plant life. But you are not likely to see the nocturnal beavers themselves.

Dana Glacier and deer

Ptarmigan in summer plumage

Carnivores hunted to rarity by man find shelter in this vast and remote mountains refuge. The Wolverine and Fisher survive here. The wolf and Grizzly bear may. Shy hunting cats like bobcat and cougar live in these mountains. But you are not likely to see even the tracks of any of these creatures. It takes many prey to feed even one hunter. The carnivores, even when they prosper, tend to be widely scattered with large hunting territories.

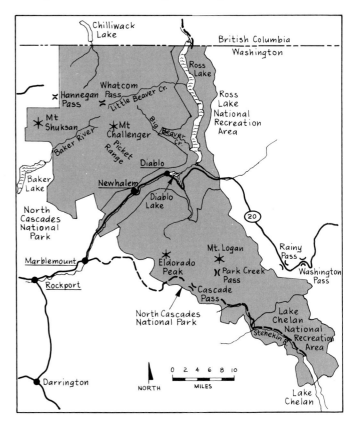

Common mergansers

19 Marblemount Eagle Sanctuary

Best season: December-February
Highlights: Bald eagles
Camping: No
Contact: Wash. St. Game Dept., Mt. Vernon
Regional Office, 1100 E. College Way,
Mt. Vernon. 206-424-1177

The edge of the Skagit River between Concrete and Marblemount is the easiest place in Washington to see the Bald eagle, the nation's symbol and a rare and endangered species. Between mid-December and mid-February, more than 100 may congregate here, feeding on the carcasses of spawned-out salmon.

Getting there is simple: You just drive east on the North Cascades Highway. Between Concrete and Marblemount, stop on turnouts along the north bank of the river and look across to the south bank with binoculars. You probably will see eagles nobly posed on bare limbs over the river—or gorging themselves and squabbling over dead salmon on the gravel bars.

The weather is often foul in their mid-December through mid-February gathering time. Happily for you, the many rainy days are best as the eagles are likely to be soaring high in the air when it is sunny. And you will get the best look by staying in your warm, dry car and not getting out and frightening the birds.

Stay on the main highway. Do not drive the road south of the river or try to walk to the bank where the eagles are. The viewing is not as good and you will only disturb the birds, lessening the chances that they will continue to gather here.

The eagle's "character" has been in dispute ever since it was chosen as the nation's symbol in 1782. Critics have pointed out that its voice is more of a cackle or squeal than a scream. Our national symbol scavenges and robs ospreys of fish they have caught. And it is something of a coward, timid about defending its nest and easily chased by smaller birds. On the other hand, the Bald eagle is a skilled fisher-bird and hunter when it cannot get food some easier way. It is hard to imagine a nobler-looking bird than this big dark hawk with white head and tail. And except for a few in far-eastern Siberia, the Bald eagle is found only in North America.

Pesticides and relentless persecution are the reasons Bald eagles have become rare. Once they were common along watercourses from sea level to subalpine heights, from the East Coast to the west. (More than half the Bald eagle's diet is fish.) But ranchers shot them for feeding on chickens and lambs; fishermen for feeding on fish; and many just killed them for thrills and target practice. The egg-shell-thinning effect of persistent pesticides and disturbance of the areas where eagles build their nests—nests five feet or more across in the tops of tall trees—contributed to the decline.

Puget Sound's first explorers found young (brown) and mature eagles common along the shores in May, 1796. But relatively few nest in the state now. Most come in the winter, probably from Canada or Alaska. They are worth looking for then along any of the state's shores, soaring proudly, flying with slow powerful wingbeats, or sitting almost immobile on a bare limb for hours, noble—but a bit boring.

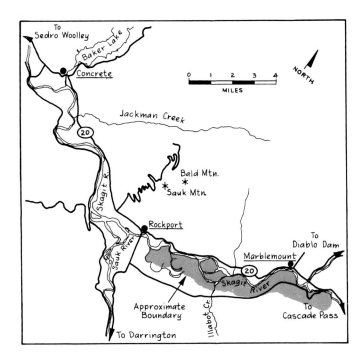

Bald eagle

55

19 Marblemount Eagle Sanctuary

Skagit River above Rockport

Bald eagles along the Skagit River

Bighorn ewe on hill a half mile above Loomis (telephoto lens foreshortens distance)

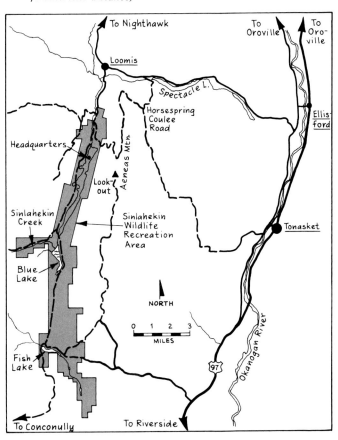

20 Sinlahekin Wildlife Recreation Area

Best season: Late winter, spring
Highlights: Deer, Bighorn sheep
Camping: Undeveloped
Contact: Wash. St. Game Dept., Regional Office, P.O. Box 1237, Ephrata, 98823. 509-754-4624

Visit Sinlahekin W.R.A. for its Bighorn sheep. Enjoy the fishing lakes in its glacial valley, and the flowers on its hillsides. Nearby, you can scramble to the top of Mt. Chopaka for a look out over the dry moonscape of the Northeast Cascades, or visit the stone ruins of a mining boom town at Nighthawk.

To reach the 13,799-acre W.R.A., drive south two miles from Loomis, or west nine miles from Highway 97 near Riverside (on the Riverside—Fish Lake Road). A good gravel road runs the length of the W.R.A.'s valley floor, past popular Blue Lake and Fish Lake, and smaller ponds.

You must head higher in the Cascades to find long hikes or tough climbs. But this area edging the mountains offers some pleasant side trips and walks. You can scramble up the valley sides, or walk an easy two miles down Coulee Creek from Fish Lake—The gulch is fragrant with flowers in spring and summer sun, and you will stumble on two ponds in the dry hills. You also can drive the road that branches north from the Fish Lake Road near the east end of Fish Lake, and follow the signs to the lookout atop Aeneas Mountain. The view is magnificent. But you may have to walk the last mile if the gate is locked.

The state bought the valley as a winter range for deer. After December it usually is hard to drive the valley road and not see deer, driven down from the highlands by deep snow.

The Bighorn sheep that are the W.R.A.'s highlight can be elusive. Deep snow sometimes brings them to the valley floor. But usually you must look for them on the slopes of Mt. Aeneas, the mountain that walls the east side of the valley. Try the walk that produced the photos here: From two miles east of Loomis, drive up Horsespring Coulee Road. Turn onto the Department of Natural Resources (D.N.R.) forest road and park where it levels off after climbing steeply. Hike up the road past the gate. You can continue for miles along a ridge, ending up at the D.N.R. fire camp if you can

Bighorn sheep (bucks) on Aeneas Mountain

arrange return transportation. The views are worth it even if you don't see sheep.

These sheep were the first California bighorns transplanted to Washington, after over-hunting, hard winters, and an epidemic of scabies brought by domestic sheep wiped out Washington's native bighorns. The 18 animals brought from British Columbia in 1957 have increased to well over 100. You may see groups of more than 40 grazing together. Most of the year, ewes, lambs, and adolescents tend to hang together—the pattern of most grazing animals, like deer and elk. Grown males prefer solitude or small groups of young-bachelor cronies.

20 Sinlahekin Wildlife Recreation Area

Chopaka Mountain from side of Aeneas Mountain

Grouse chick

Lewis' woodpecker

Mule deer

Aspen grove on Aeneas Mountain

Gardner Mountain and Methow Valley

Snowbrush   *Cat's ear (also known as sego lily)*

21 Methow
Wildlife Recreation Area

Best season: Late winter, spring
Highlights: Deer, songbirds, raptors
Camping: Adj. state park
Contact: Wash. St. Game Dept., Regional Of-
fice, P.O. Box 1237, Ephrata, 98823.
509-754-4624

This 17-mile-long strip of rolling-to-rugged rocks and pines was bought as a safety zone for deer, between the heavy snows of the adjacent National Forest and farmers' orchards and fields. It is part of the deer's traditional migration route between high mountains and valley. For other animals, it is a sort of transition area between mountain and lowland habitats, with water and steep rocks thrown in. As a result, you can see an unusual variety of species here.

To get there, take the North Cascades Highway to Twisp or Winthrop. Then take the road on the west side of the river, paralleling the highway, between the two towns. (There is good birdwatching along this quieter road itself.) Take the road where signs point you to Davis Lake and the golf course. It takes you to the W.R.A. and you can follow the signs to headquarters. The road from Pearrygin Lake State Park is closed in winter.

Deer stay in the area all winter, but late March or April often is the best time to see them. Roads are passable then. May and June are the best times for wildflowers and songbirds in this fairly high North Washington country.

There are developed camping facilities in Pearrygin Lake State Park. Camping is allowed in the W.R.A.

Birdwatchers will find the area of interest for its mixture of species. You can see birds of the high mountains—like Clark's nutcracker—and of dry foothill country—like Lewis' woodpecker. Both scold you vigorously.

There is the same sort of mixture of wildlife. Squirrels here are Red squirrels, one of the Rocky Mountain species that has a range reaching into Eastern Washington and across the highlands on the north edge of the state to the Cascades.

This sort of rocky country is good habitat for Washington's wild cats, especially Bobcat. Although these short-tailed, spotted cats about a yard long actually are fairly common in much of the state, they are largely nocturnal and so quiet, well-camouflaged, and adept at hiding in trees or rocks that you are not likely to see one. They eat mostly mice, rabbits, and other small animals, and are no threat to you.

Pine branch at pollination time

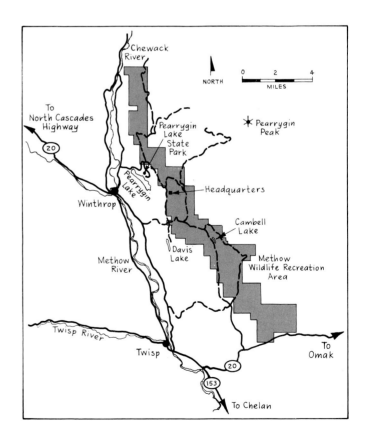

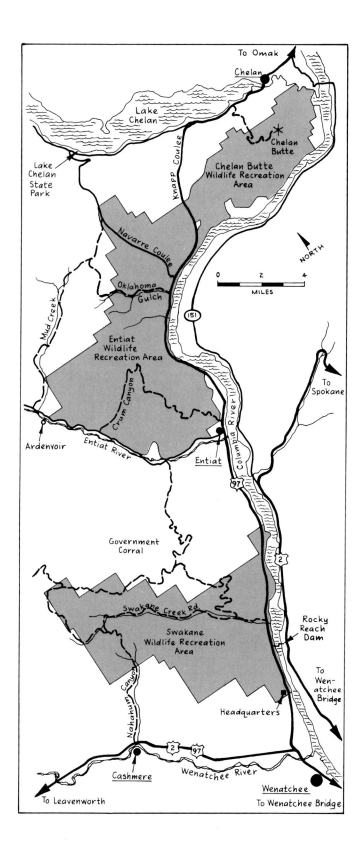

22 Entiat Mountains
Swankane, Entiat and Chelan Butte Wildlife Recreation Areas

Best season: Late winter, spring
Highlights: Deer, song-birds, wildflowers
Camping: Undeveloped
Contact: Wash. St. Game Dept., Regional Office, 2802 Naches Highway, Yakima, 98902. 509-248-5832

Swankane, Entiat, and Chelan Butte W.R.A.s, on the dry east edge of the Cascades north of Wenatchee, offer you rare wildflowers, spectacular views, the easy-to-watch wildlife of open foothills and canyons, and the winter home of almost 8,000 mule deer.

All three are just off State Highway 97 between Wenatchee and Chelan. A mile north of Rocky Reach Dam on the Columbia, Swakane Creek Road leads you west into 11,838-acre Swakane W.R.A. Roads leading north from the road to Ardenvoir and west from Highway 97 take you into Entiat W.R.A.'s 10,883 acres a few miles to the north. From both, you can continue higher into the Wenatchee National Forest.

At the south edge of the town of Chelan, the road to Chelan Butte Fire Lookout winds up into the 3,170-acre Chelan Butte W.R.A.

These relatively small W.R.A.s are places to visit for a few hours or a day, perhaps on your way to the nearby national forest or Lake Chelan. The W.R.A.s do not have developed camping areas. They offer short walks up canyons and hillsides, but no long hikes. The best time for a visit is Spring—late April through June—when the wildflowers are in bloom and the birds and mammals are most active. But anytime except noisy hunting season is pleasant. When snow is heavy, the roads make a good snowshoe or cross-country-ski trip.

Swakane is best known for its wildflowers: This area is the only known home of a little pinkish-red clover called Thompson's clover. This also is one of the places you can see the rare and endangered Lewisia tweedyi. Look at but don't dig or pick its desert-gray leaves and dawn-flushed flowers. A main reason this plant is in danger of extinction is that too many have picked its blooms or taken the plants home to their gardens, where they usually die.

Swakane also has a small herd of Bighorn sheep. Drive about three miles into the W.R.A. from Highway 97 and look up on the hillside north of the road.

The hillside above Highway 97 is as likely a place as any to see the deer that migrate here in winter. You can find the gnawed limbs and droppings under trees that tell you that porcupines, uncommon west of the mountains, live in the pines here. In more open country there are signs of badgers. Chipmunks "whisk"-ing at you are not Townsend's, as they are west of the Cascades, but Yellow-pine chipmunks.

Chelan Butte W.R.A. has a magnificent view of the Columbia winding out to desert and wheatlands and Lake Chelan snaking up to the icy North Cascades. Look in the sky for Golden eagles, and in nearby pines for Lewis woodpeckers, the fly-catching woodpeckers of the desert, in black suits, gray collars, and pinkish vests. Expect Valley quail and Chukar partridges if you walk the blooming hillside in spring. These two transplanted game birds have thrived here.

Mule deer

Evening grosbeak

Tweedy's lewisia

Lake Chelan from Chelan Butte

Bald eagle and magpie sharing a roadkill beside the Columbia River

67

Elk cow

23 Colockum
Wildlife Recreation Area

Best season: Spring
Highlights: Elk, songbirds; wildflowers
Camping: Undeveloped
Contact: Wash. St. Game Dept., Regional Office, 2802 Naches Highway, Yakima, 98902. 509-248-5832

This 115,768-acre state game range rolls from the Columbia River and its desert canyon up to piney, 6,878-foot Mission Peak in the Wenatchee Mountains. You can explore wildlife communities from mountain to desert on its extensive, though rough, network of dirt roads. Or camp, and take short hikes up open hills or along canyons.

Dirt roads marked with W.R.A. signs run east or west from the old Colockum Pass Road, an old Indian trail and stagecoach route. You can reach the Colockum Pass Road going south from Malaga, or north from Kittitas on Road 81 and east on Erickson Road. (You may not be able to cross the pass in an ordinary car.)

To reach the separate southeast portion of the W.R.A., take the old highway between Kittitas and Vantage. A W.R.A. sign takes you up the Whiskey Dick Creek Road. You go up into dry sage-and-cactus hills, down into oasis-like stream canyons noisy with birds in spring, out to the Columbia where swallows dart from the cliffs and ducks and geese rest spring and fall.

One of the best wildlife-watching spots is not even in the W.R.A. From the overlook at Trinidad, just off State Highway 28 between Wenatchee and Quincy, you can look across with binoculars or telescope at West Bar on the Columbia and have a fair chance of seeing one of the W.R.A.'s small herds of Pronghorn antelope. (Another herd hangs out in the dry southeast segment, around Saddle Mountain.) Hundreds of elk, too, winter on the bar or above it in the hills around Tarpiscan Creek.

But if you don't see Colockum's pronghorns, elk, deer, or Bighorn sheep, you will still go home enriched by a spring or summer trip. There are the intense fragrances of this sunny country—pine, sage, mint in the stream canyons. There is the white veil of bloom of wild cherries and serviceberry along the streams in spring, ripening to the dark berries Indians used for pemmican (and you can use for jelly).

And there is the concentration of life in these same stream canyons, where animals of pine forest and desert hills mix with those of brush and cottonwood and water. Yellow-pine chipmunks or Rock wrens scold you from heaps of lichen-crusted lava. Mourning doves hoot across the canyons. The

bright birds of cottonwoods and streamside brush can be cheerful—like the blue Lazuli bunting or the red-and-yellow Western tanager—or raucous with the chatter of fluorescent-orange-and-black Bullock's orioles and the Yellow-breasted chat, catcalling between mellow whistles. You can find yourself with the desert's Western meadowlarks and Lark sparrows in the sage on one side; and a little swamp colony of Killdeer, Snipe, and Red-winged blackbirds on the other.

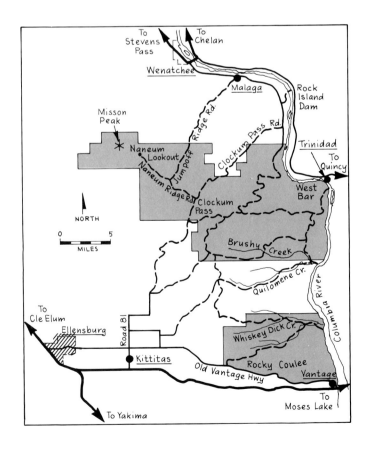

Female White-headed woodpecker

Mourning doves

Elk cows   *Mule deer*

Yellow bell   Shooting star   Grass widow

Columbia River above West Bar

24 Oak Creek
Oak Creek and L.T. Murray
Wildlife Recreation Areas

Best season: Spring
Highlights: Elk, songbirds; wildflowers
Camping: Undeveloped
Contact: Wash. St. Game Dept., Regional Office, 2802 Naches Highway, Yakima, 98902. 509-248-5832

These adjacent state game areas, totalling more than 200,000 acres, roll down the southeast edge of the Cascades from pine forests and flowery hilltop balds, through lava canyons that echo with the "tom-toms" of drumming Blue grouse in spring, to bare hills of sage and grass where you can watch hawks soar and young coyotes learn to hunt.

You can hike, camp, or explore by car driving old stagecoach roads and discovering abandoned homesteads where dooryard lilacs still bloom.

Wildlife watching here is excellent, for two main reasons: The mixture of broken woods, brush, water, and open country on this edge of the mountains provides varied habitat to suit many kinds of birds and animals. And because the country is fairly open, you can see what is around you.

The best time for a visit may be spring. By May and June the roads usually are dry. Through July, the ground is bright with flowers.

The area is easy to reach from the major cross-Cascade highways: Interstate 90 across Snoqualmie Pass, State Highway 410 across Chinook Pass, or U.S. 12 across White Pass.

The Taneum Creek Road exit from Interstate 90 (exit 93, about 13 miles west of Ellensburg) lets you wander up through piney hills where hilltop meadows—like those at Tamarack Springs—give you dramatic views of the Cascades and castle-like Mt. Stuart. Here the animals are still those of mountain pine forests: Rattling White-headed woodpeckers like death in a black robe; Pine grosbeaks in yellow, black and white formal attire, giving mellow whistles and warbles. Notice how these birds are built for their "jobs": The grosbeak's stout bill helps open stubborn cones. The woodpecker's stubby tail and one back-turned claw help brace him on trunks. His bill is built to chisel.

Each road here is a discovery: Robinson Canyon with its dramatic lava cliffs; the old log buildings in the "Gopher Hole" on Watt Canyon; the old Durr stage road that takes you high on bare hills where meadowlarks sing; suddenly down into Umptanum Canyon where you snack on currants beside a cool creek and watch Lewis woodpeckers, or a badger hurrying away; up again and over the hills to Yakima. (Take Wenas Road and Sheep Road from Selah to reach the Durr Road from the south end.)

There is good walking in the area, too. From the cable bridge crossing the Yakima River between miles 16 and 17 on State Highway 181 (the old highway through the canyon) you can hike 10 miles on the Umptanum Trail to the old Wenas-Ellensburg Road, another old wagon route. Carry your own water and stove. Fires are not allowed in the dry hills in summer. The Cleman Mountain area north of Highway 410 is closed to motor vehicles in part, and there is good walking on its bare, dry slopes cut with knife-like lava outcrops.

The southern part of the area is just as interesting, with dramatic Bear Canyon, and easy springtime walks from roads like Oak Creek and Bethel Ridge. Explore the stream canyons with their intense concentrations of life.

Oak Creek also has a winter attraction: At the headquarters just off the White Pass Highway, about two miles west of its junction with 410, you can watch hundreds of elk munching on hay the Game Department feeds them to keep them from invading the farms and orchards that now occupy their ancestral wintering grounds. As feeding times may vary, and light snows may mean the elk are not there at all, check with headquarters if you want to be sure to see them.

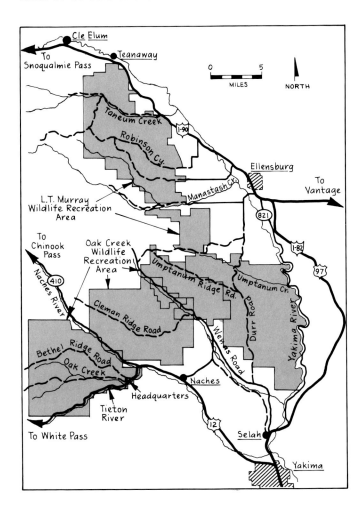

Elk in the Oak Creek feed lot

Magpie

Mountain bluebird

Mount Stuart Range from Manastash Ridge

Oak Creek and L.T. Murray Wildlife Recreation Areas

Elk in the Oak Creek feed lot

Long-plumed avens   *Glacier lily (dogtooth violet)*   *Yellow paintbrush*

Toad

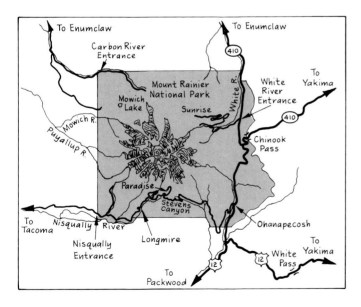

25 Mount Rainier National Park

Best season: Summer
Highlights: Deer, elk, ptarmigan; wild-
flowers, backpacking, climbing
Camping: Yes
Contact: Park Supt., Mt. Rainier Natl. Park,
Longmire, Wa., 98397. 206-569-2343

Mt. Rainier itself, at 14,410 feet the tallest of Cascade volcanos, is the park's chief attraction, of course. Next come its vast glaciers and its alpine meadows, with their quick-changing wildflower show from July through September. There are evergreen forests floored with moss, ferns, and white wildflowers. Knowing and watching the park's wildlife will add to your enjoyment, no matter what you come to see.

Some animals will be familiar: the deer that graze year-round near the Nisqually entrance station, the high-voiced Pikas and Hoary marmots that greet hikers at alpine rock slides, the Yellow-pine chipmunks and Golden-mantled ground squirrels that forage in high meadows—and beg in picnic areas. (In case you are not sure which of these you are seeing, the chipmunk's stripes go through his eye and the ground squirrel's do not.)

One of Rainier's herds of mountain goats wanders near Panhandle Gap. Others live on the heights of Emerald Ridge and Indian Henry's Hunting Ground. If you drive in at the Nisqually Entrance Station in winter, look for them on the cliffs high above the road between Tahoma and Kautz Creeks.

The park's big animals are nothing to be afraid of, although it pays to be aware of potential trouble. Here as anywhere in the mountains there are cougar. But these big shy cats will not attack you—Count yourself lucky if you see one. Black bear are fairly common sights, and usually will run from you, especially if you make noise. But give them a wide berth if you meet one—in a campground, or feasting on high-country blueberries. Elk, once almost wiped out in the Cascades, are now flourishing in such numbers that they are overgrazing parts of the park. Cowlitz Divide is a likely place to see them. But in their fall "rut" or mating season they can be dangerous. Listen to their "bugling" from a distance, but stay away.

Here as everywhere, birds are the animals you see and hear most often. Knowing the birds around you helps you realize how life changes as you move up and down the mountains.

In the dark everygreen forests, learn to listen for birds you may not see: Winter wrens almost whispering their rapid songs near the forest floor; Pine siskins and Red crossbills, vagabonds that follow the cone crops, moving in flocks through the treetops.

At the edges of streams and lakes, Spotted sandpipers bob and complain, and the dark, short-tailed Dipper walks underwater for food, or bobs and sings on rocks.

High up where forests begin to thin out are typical high-mountain species: Clark's nutcracker, Hermit thrush, Mountain chickadee, Mountain bluebird. Northern three-toed woodpecker.

Higher still you can see the few birds that nest in the rock gardens above timberline: the Gray-crowned rosy finch, the bobbing Water pipit; and—if you are lucky and hike in the early morning—little flocks of White-tailed ptarmigan scurrying along trails. With feathered legs and broad snowshoe-like feet, they stay year round, turning white in winter.

Avalanche lilies and Mount Rainier

Beargrass

Seed pods of the Western anemone

Avalanche lily

Steller's jay

Clark's nutcracker

Hoary marmot

Golden-mantled ground squirrel

Mountain goats at Panhandle Gap

Canada geese

Canada geese on guard at Conboy

26 Conboy Lake National Wildlife Refuge

Best season: Late winter, spring
Highlights: Canada geese, beaver colony
Camping: No
Contact: Refuge Mgr., Rt. 1, Box 1300, Toppenish, 98948. 509-865-2405

Tumbledown farmhouses and weathered barns on pine-fringed fields; the gentle South Cascades folding back in green and blue; and snow-capped Mt. Adams towering over all; make a visit to this high, cold plateau worthwhile even if it had no wildlife. When hordes of migrant geese and ducks wheel and call in this mountain setting, it takes on magic.

From State Highway 14 about 60 miles east of Vancouver, turn north on State Highway 141, through White Salmon. Ten miles north on State Highway 141, at B-Z Corner, turn northeast onto the Glenwood Road. Nine miles farther on, the road hits the refuge, skirts its east boundary for about seven miles, and continues about 1½ miles into the little town of Glenwood.

You also can drive about 30 miles from Goldendale on the Glenwood Road. This route takes you through the spectacular Klickitat Canyon and W.R.A., a good place to camp year-round. In summer you may want to continue to Trout Lake and the spectacular wildflower show at Bird Creek Meadows on the Yakima Indian Reservation. (The tribe may charge admission.)

Conboy does not offer outhouses, running water, or other public facilities. Camping is forbidden. Perhaps the best wildlife viewing is from the roads edging the refuge: Much of the interior is closed and flooded in winter and at the height of spring migration. You can walk and picnic in the fields and pine groves near the north end. And from an overgrown road marked "No Vehicles" less than a quarter mile from refuge headquarters, you can follow plastic ribbons marking an easy, 3½-mile round-trip walk to a beaver colony at Willard Springs.

The refuge has a curious history. It was a shallow lake that should have belonged to the Yakima Indians. But whites conveniently lost the treaty maps. Settlers moved in and drained the lake for fields, letting it fill up again only in winter. Now the federal government is trying to buy enough land to bring the lake back to life and manage it for ducks and geese. So far, it has not succeeded: Descendants of some of the settlers are putting up stiff resistance.

Conboy's mountain-rimmed remnants of lake and farms are worth a visit any time of year. But they may be most fascinating in early spring—late

Bird Creek Meadows and Mount Adams

February through April—when the refuge may seem to belong to you and thousands of migrant waterbirds. Dusky tones of Candada geese harmonize with still-brown fields and gray sky. The Mallards, bowing and whistling in courtship, are a touch of spring green with their irridescent heads. Hawks not yet gone back to the mountains to nest hunt from pines and fence posts: Mice displaced by the seasonal flooding may make easy prey. Great blue herons, too, stalk the temporary lake and flooded fields. At dusk, watch for deer and hares coming out of daytime hiding.

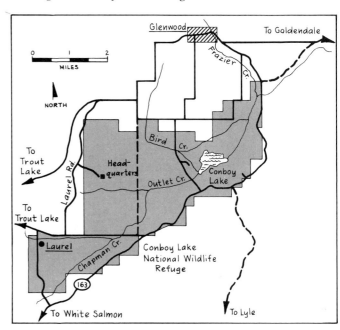

27 Klickitat Wildlife Recreation Area

Best season: Spring
Highlights: Deer, Vaux swifts, songbirds, gamebirds, squirrels
Camping: Yes
Contact: Wash. St. Game Dept., Regional Office, 2802 Naches Highway, Yakima, 98902. 509-248-5832

The spectacular canyon of the Klickitat, with pines and oak groves scattered down its sides and views of Mt. Adams and Mt. Hood from meadows at its rim, is reason enough to visit this 13,000-acre state game area. Black-tailed deer that come down from higher mountains in winter; easy songbird-watching in the open woods in spring and summer; and some unusual animal inhabitants make it special any time of year.

To get there, drive about nine miles east from Klickitat or west from Goldendale on State Highway 142, and turn north on the Glenwood Road. About three miles north of the junction the first of several dirt roads leads west into the W.R.A. Be cautious on these roads: They are rough at best. Most quickly drop from the pine flats you see to steep canyon sides. And when they are wet in winter and spring they turn to treacherously slippery mud.

About a half mile past the road to Soda Springs—one of many mineral springs edging the river in this volcanic land—a short spur road with a W.R.A. sign leads to headquarters.

About a mile further you come with breath-taking suddenness to the rim of the deep, winding canyon the Klickitat River has cut in the South Cascade lavas. The canyon's V-shape is quite unlike the U-profile of many Cascade valleys cut by glaciers: Ice Age glaciers did not reach this far south.

The road winds down to campgrounds on the river that make this W.R.A. a good place for camping almost year-round. They usually are snow-free by March.

There are no developed trails. But walking is easy in the open woods, and you can scramble along the river.

The W.R.A. has the typical wildlife of the Southeast Cascades, plus some unusual features.

Flocks of Band-tailed pigeons visit the canyon winter and spring as if it were a resort: They appear morning and evening to drink from the mineral springs along the river.

The abandoned Mineral Springs Bottling Works on the river at the town of Klickitat makes an interesting little satellite of the W.R.A.: A colony of Vaux's swifts lives there in summer, and you can watch them diving nimbly down the chimney.

Deer grazing below Mount Adams

Waterfall just off the Glenwood Road

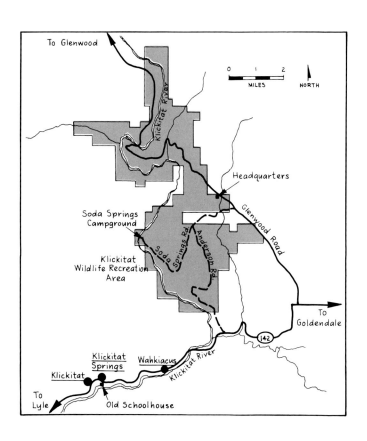

Banks Reservoir

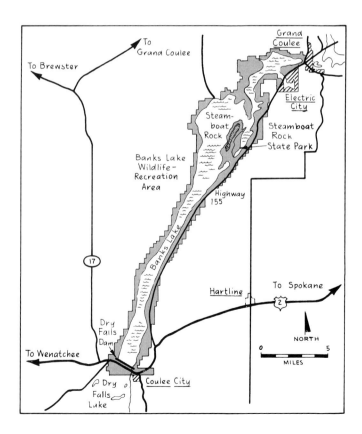

28 Banks Lake
Wildlife Recreation Area

Best season: Early fall, late winter, spring
Highlights: Water birds, shore birds, gulls;
         wildflowers, Steamboat Rock
Camping: Yes
Contact: Wash. St. Game Dept., Regional Of-
         fice, P.O. Box 1237, Ephrata, 98823.
         509-754-4624

Like most Central Washington wildlife areas, Banks Lake presents you with a contrast that is partly man-made. The W.R.A. is a narrow strip of canyon wall, greasewood and sage edging a 27-mile-long irrigation reservoir. The result is a rather startling mixture of desert and water life: a juxtaposition you can enjoy in many places in the canyon-cut plateau of the Columbia Basin in Central Washington.

Highway 155 between Coulee City and Grand Coulee runs through the W.R.A. between the canyon wall and the lake. (Coulee City is about 63 miles northeast of Wenatchee on U.S. 2.)

You can camp in Steamboat Rock State Park just off the highway. The cliffs limit hiking, but there are places where you can scramble safely to the ridge top for sweeping views and a look at desert life. A good trail leads to the top of Steamboat Rock: It is marked only by a "Keep Out" sign that refers to a sewage-disposal pond. But you can find it by looking for the only break in the otherwise vertical cliffs.

As in most of this desert country, spring is the best time for a visit—roughly from April through June. Waterfalls hang in plumes from the cliffs; wildflowers are in bloom; waterbirds, gulls, and shorebirds are migrating through or settling in to nest. The desert's birds are singing, and its rodents have not yet gone into their summer sleep.

Although each area has its distinctive mixture, much the same species of birds and mammals are found in most of these sage and grasslands cut by lava canyons and rock outcrops called scablands. Their geological history is similar, too. Quiet flows of lava 15 million years ago and more built the Columbia Plateau. The hills rose later: The meandering canyons of the Yakima and the Grande Ronde show the rivers once wound over a flat plain and kept the course as the hills rose. Much more recently, a lobe of the Ice Age ice sheet from Canada reached south along the Cascades as far as Waterville, and pushed the Columbia south to cut the canyon that now holds Banks Lake. But this alone does not account for the Grand Coulee, as the canyon is called—27 miles long, 400 feet deep, and in places four miles wide. The ice sheets also dammed a lake that held as much as 50 cubic miles of water in Idaho and Montana. When the dam broke, this

Canada goose

lake drained west across the Columbia Plateau and out to the Pacific via the Columbia Gorge in less than two weeks. This may have been repeated seven times or more. These floods cut the Grand Coulee, with its huge dry waterfalls; and the other dry coulees walled by the layered basalt of the old lava flows, cracked into six-sided columns as it cooled.

The retreat of the glacier some 12,000 years ago let the Columbia go back to its old course. Man wrote the final chapter, building Grand Coulee Dam in the 1930s, and other dams; filling the old flood canyons with irrigation water. The irrigation water in turn seeped out to form smaller pothole lakes in sinks swept out by the ancient flood waters.

Trail sign

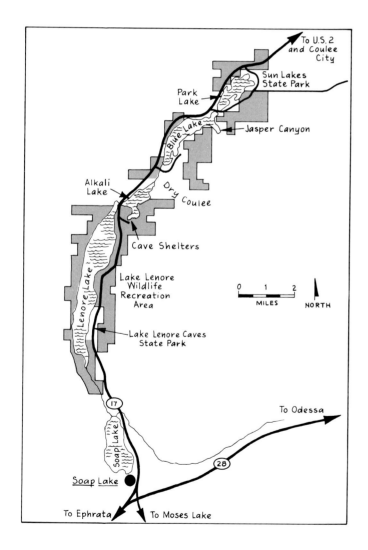

29 Lenore Lake Area

Best season: Early fall, late winter, spring
Highlights: Water birds, shorebirds, wild-
    flowers, Dry Falls, rock shelters
Camping: Adjacent state park
Contact: Wash. St. Game Dept., Regional Of-
    fice, P.O. Box 1237, Ephrata, 98823.
    509-754-4624

Lenore Lake Wildlife Recreation Area and the neighboring Sun Lakes lie in the lower Grand Coulee, below Dry Falls—cliffs that were a 400-foot, three-mile-wide waterfall when Ice Age floods carved the 27-mile-long canyon and swept the nearby scablands bare of topsoil.

The interpretive center beside the highway above the falls, near Sun Lakes State Park, is a "must" stop for its displays and explanation of the area's fascinating natural history—including rock shelters used by Indian hunting parties, and the lava cast of a prehistoric rhinoceros. A sign on the paved side road near the north end of Lenore Lake directs you to a short trail to several of the rock shelters themselves.

The lakes themselves, with the fall, winter, and spring birds that are the area's main wildlife attraction, are easy to reach. State Highway 17 north of the resort town of Soap Lake edges Lenore, Soap, Blue, and some of the other lakes. The road to the camping area at Sun Lakes State Park also lets you drive near the pothole lakes on the coulee floor, with good birdwatching from the "blind" of your car.

The wildlife here is typical of the many lakes in the Central Washington desert. But it may surprise you if you have not watched life in this area before. Seagulls, for example, nest in this area (not the Glaucous-winged gulls that nest on offshore rocks in Western Washington, but smaller Ring-billed and California gulls). Nimble Forster's terns give rusty little cries as they hover and dip. They are another seabird that comes to the desert to nest, usually in island colonies.

In the marshes, Red-winged blackbirds familiar from Western Washington honk at you. And Yellow-headed blackbirds in colonies in the rushes make enough noise for a whole city traffic jam when you come near.

Spring and fall, migrating shorebirds wade on their long legs and probe with their long bills the lakeshores here, as they do in Western Washington beaches. But they are generally different species: Long-billed dowitchers instead of the Short-billed more common in Western Washington; black, white, and shell-pink Avocets almost unknown west of the Cascades; and others.

Flower fields near Lake Lenore

The Canada geese grazing in the fields here are of different subspecies than those in Western Washington, although it would take an expert to tell the difference. The spectrum of ducks that migrates through and winters or nests in the area is different from that in Western Washington. Salt-water ducks, like scoters that dive for shellfish they swallow whole, are rare. The Green-winged (or Common) teal usually seen west of the Cascades are joined by many Blue-winged and Cinnamon teal. Here as in Western Washington, though, each body of water gets its own characteristic "mix" of waterbirds, depending on the kinds of food and protection it provides. Each species has its own demands.

Look up for the birds of cliffs, too: The noisily twittering, quickly wheeling Cliff swallows and White-throated swifts that nest here. The Cliff swallows stick egg-shaped nests made of mud pellets to the cliffs. Swifts gluing feathers and down together with their spittle in cracks in the rock. Both hunt insects on the wing with short, wide beaks built for the job.

Summer Falls and Billy Clapp Lake (reservoir)

30 Long Lake Area
Stratford and Long Lake Wildlife Recreation Areas

Best season: Early fall, late winter, spring
Highlights: Canada geese
Camping: No
Contact: Wash. St. Game Dept., Regional Office, P.O. Box 1237, Ephrata, 98823. 509-754-4624

Bitterroot

At these reservoirs edged by desert, you can enjoy the bluffs and scablands in their brief spring bloom. Cool off at Summer Falls. And get to know the Canada geese that have found the flooded coulee a prime place to rest and nest.

To get there, drive ten miles east from Soap Lake on State Highway 28. Stratford Lake, the small reservoir at the W.R.A.'s south end is just north of the highway. A spur road just west of the lake leads about two miles to a parking area, boat launch, and rest rooms on the main reservoir. Summer Falls State Park at the north end of the main reservoir can be reached by taking Pinto Ridge Road north from Highway 28 or south from Coulee City. Signs for the falls and park mark the way.

There are no developed camping areas. The falls is a cooling stop for a picnic in the hot Central Washington summer: The constant breeze often brings spray onto the park lawn. But the grass is too civilized for much wildlife besides the barn swallows that nest fearlessly under the picnic-shelter eaves and chirp angrily at intruding humans.

Stratford Lake lets you watch waterbirds, especially Canada geese, almost from the highway in winter and spring. Geese winter and nest here. Mated for life, they begin to move in pairs in early spring. While nesting is underway, you may see the gander, on guard near where the female is incubating eggs. Even when the flocks re-unite about July, though, and while adults are flightless during their molt, you often can spot family groups, for parents and offspring swim about and graze together.

With geese as with other birds it is nice to know a bit of the "language" and "social customs"—the head-bobbing that is a signal that the bird is about to fly (the bobbing bird may wait until his partner or family bobs with him, and then all take off), the erect necks of geese on watch, usually on the outskirts of grazing flocks; the hissing rushes that usually mean one goose is setting straight another that violated the flock's rank order.

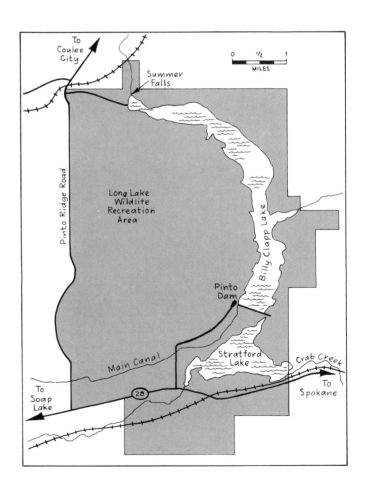

89

Cattail marsh

Spring-fed tributary of Crab Creek

Duck's nest

American avocet

31 Gloyd Seeps
Wildlife Recreation Area

Best season: Spring
Highlights: Waterbirds, shorebirds, songbirds
Camping: Undeveloped
Contact: Wash. St. Game Dept., Regional Office, P.O. Box 1237, Ephrata, 98823. 509-754-4624

Common snipe

Stop at Gloyd Seeps for a few hours in spring and discover a bird watcher's small paradise. The W.R.A.'s 9,733 acres mix low lava toes, marsh, salt flats, sage desert, ponds, and streams. It has birds to match them all. The barely rolling, 11-mile strip along Crab Creek is not spectacular—you are seldom out of sight of farms, and planes leaving nearby Grant County Airport disturb your peace. But you will soon be fascinated by the intensity of the life that crowds a watery "oasis" in the desert.

From State Highway 17 near the north end of the town of Moses Lake, take the road to Stratford. This road becomes J Street Northeast. To reach the main refuge, turn west onto 12th, 14th, or 16th Northeast to one of three parking lots.

It is natural springs or "seeps" in the desert that give this area its odd-sounding name. You can spend a magic afternoon at one of them—a little pond fringed with bright yellow-green swamp grass and half-dead willows, a bright spot in the gray sage. Be still and more colors and sounds crowd around you.

You see the songbirds of desert, marsh, and streamside brush and trees: a Scarlet tanager, bright red head over sun-yellow body; a fluorescent orange Bullock's oriole; bright yellow, black capped Wilson's warblers; red-winged and yellow-headed blackbirds; the yellow-flushed Western meadowlark.

A pair of kingbirds, the gray and white flycatchers that seem to rule almost every Eastern Washington pond, dart from a snag after flies. They show how they got their name by chasing away other birds that come near. A Killdeer tries to lead you away with plaints and flutters. A half-dozen teal and Shoveler ducks stir the shallow pond bottom with their broad bills. The Shovelers look quite comic paddling in circles with their heads under water.

A dome of dried grass tells you muskrats lodge here. What looks like bundles of sticks in the willows say the pond is also a magpie nesting colony. The parents sneaked away silently as you approached and now are scavenging over the desert, looking like birds of paradise with their long tails. The youngsters, already out of their roofed nests, watch you warily from a well-hidden branch. Although magpies are known for stealing other birds'

eggs and young, they obviously have not discouraged the many other songbirds here. And the magpies compensate for the damage they do, in a way: Other birds roost in their abandoned nests or even lay eggs in them.

Over the whole tiny oasis hangs the faint smell of death: The body of a rattlesnake is a reminder of death and danger even in this peace.

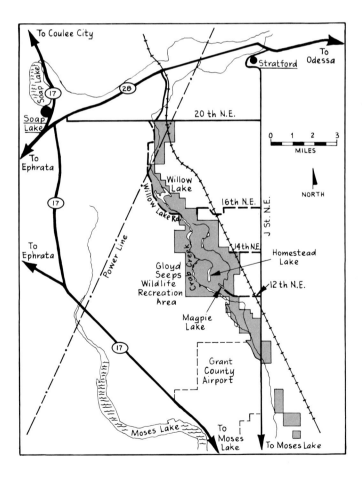

91

Basalt pillars on old U.S. 10

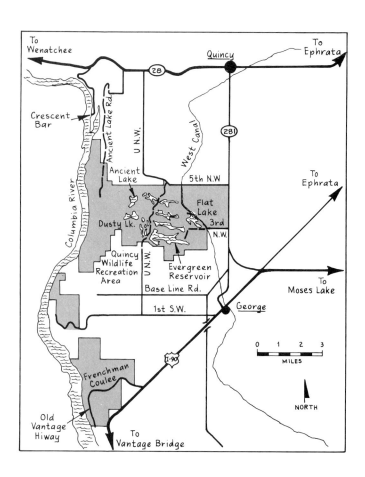

32 Quincy Wildlife Recreation Area

Best season: Spring
Highlights: Waterbirds, shorebirds; wild-
flowers, views
Camping: Undeveloped
Contact: Wash. St. Game Dept., Regional Of-
fice, P.O. Box 1237, Ephrata, 98823.
509-754-4624

This 13,508 acre wildlife recreation area offers you 25 pothole lakes, views from the Columbia canyon's rim that are almost frightening—and the wildlife of the irrigated Central Washington desert.

Quincy W.R.A. lies along and north of Interstate Highway 90 just east of the bridge that crosses the Columbia canyon at Vantage. For easy access to spectacular views, drive to the separate viewpoints provided for eastbound and westbound freeway traffic. Or take old U.S. 10, that winds down Frenchman Coulee north of the freeway to the now-drowned site of the old Vantage bridge. For more solitude, you can take the Ancient Lake Road that runs south from State Highway 28 between Quincy and Crescent Bar. The road deteriorates into jeep tracks. But you can walk to the canyon rim or to some of the less used brushy coulees and small lakes.

For easy access to parking areas on the shores of the larger lakes, take County Road 3 or 5 Northwest west from State Highway 281 between George and Quincy. Or take Base Line Road west from 281 just north of the freeway, and turn north on U Northwest to reach the W.R.A.

The area is busy with fishermen in summer and hunters in fall. Spring is the best time for a visit, with migration and nesting underway.

Cliff swallows swirl like swarms of bees and chirp rustily as they fight for possession of last year's nests on the cliffs above the Columbia. Clouds of Red-winged and Yellow-headed blackbirds return to the ready spots. Males arrive first, staking out separate colonies for each species and individual territories within those. The later-arriving females are courted with ringing calls and absurdly awkward bows and hunched flights designed to show the males' gala shoulder markings. But when the male has won a bride—or two or three, for the birds are polygamous—he leaves her to do all the work of building the nest and rearing young. Males are aggressive guards, though. They will mob and chase crows, gulls, and hawks—and buzz and dive-bomb you if you come too close to their nests.

Look for the Whistling swans that rest here each spring along with Canada geese and more than a dozen kinds of ducks, carrying on their courtships as they move north.

Along with the native desert birds, look for the game birds introduced by hunting enthusiasts and prospering as irrigation and farming spread: the Ring-necked pheasant from China, males gala with irridescent heads and long trailing tail; and the Chukar partridge all the way from India, tan face gravely ringed and masked in black. These plump birds walk about and peck for food on the ground much like chickens. In spring you can hear the males crowing or calling "chu-kar"—You may spot one on a low promontory. After the eggs hatch (the nest usually is on the ground under the shelter of a bush) you may see the females leading their broods and hear "conversations" of ticks and clubks that mean things like "get the flock together" or "stay under cover."

A seep lake

93

33 Upper Potholes Area
Potholes, Winchester and Desert Wildlife Recreation Areas

Best season: Spring
Highlights: Shorebirds, waterbirds; canoeing
Camping: Adjacent state park
Contact: Wash. St. Game Dept., Regional Office, P.O. Box 1237, Ephrata, 98823. 509-754-4624

Canoe, if you can, this vast complex of gray-green sage and blue-gray water totalling more than 60,000 acres. Or just stop your car and rest, watching quiet desert and water with a cushion of cattails or willows in between.

These three wildlife-recreation areas—Desert, Winchester, and Potholes—lie south and west of the city of Moses Lake, where irrigation reservoirs and big wasteways cut low sand dunes. From Interstate 90, you can take the Moses Lake State Park exit or the Dodson Road exit 10 miles west of Moses Lake. Dirt roads running south from the road paralleling the freeway on the south take you to the north part of the reservoir. From Dodson Road you can go north and west to three miles of easy canoeing on the Winchester Wasteway north of the freeway, where rushes are filled with blackbirds, marsh wrens, and nesting Blue-winged and Cinnamon teal. Or go south on Dodson to cross Winchester Wasteway and Frenchman Hills Lake and Wasteway. The Frenchman Hills-O'Sullivan Road, running along the south side of the wildlife area, has spurs and places where you can pull off, launch a small boat and paddle or just walk a bit, enjoying the life of desert and water. But beware of culverts and falls.

For the best wildlife watching, stay away from the southeast part of the main reservoir, near O'Sullivan Dam. It is a playground for motorboats, with fishing resorts and a state park with camping. Go instead to the less-used maze of channels and half-drowned sand dunes in the northwest part of the reservoir. (But be prepared to wade and push your boat through shallow spots, and be careful not to get lost.)

As you explore the quiet waterways, keep an eye out for water mammals—muskrat, beaver, an occasional mink. You may see jackrabbits, coyotes, even a deer on shore, especially near dusk. Ducks and geese rest and nest here in abundance. Gulls and terns rear their young near desert shores—usually in nesting colonies on islands. Like the colonies of nesting Red-winged and Yellow-headed blackbirds, they protest your approach with noisy alarms.

Stilt-legged Great blue herons hunt along the shallow shores, as do Black-crowned night herons, stocky, short-necked, dull-colored and small. But

Long-billed curlew

the night herons fish mostly between dusk and dawn. You are more likely to hear their croaking "quawk" than to see them. You may spot the White pelican, a big white bird with black-tipped wings and heavy orange bill and legs. It rests in these and other East Central Washington waterways on migration.

Look, too, for the shorebirds, whose enlongated legs and bills fit them for wading and probing in sand and mud for small prey. There probably is no better place for watching them.

The Avocets look like china figurines with their sleek black-and-white bodies, flesh-pink heads, stilt-like legs and slim upcurbed bills. Skittering and poking near them may be the much smaller Wilson's phalaropes, birds that have reversed the usual sex roles. The brighter colored females do the courting. The dull-gray and brown male builds the nest and incubates the eggs while the female stands guard nearby. Here, too, you will see the Long-billed curlew, largest of North American shorebirds—a big brown bird whose four-inch-long bill curves downward. (If it is straight or curves up, you are seeing a godwit, another of these birds whose odd names are supposed to resemble their calls.)

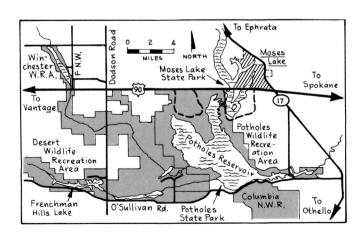

Sand dock in dunes

Yellow-headed blackbird

Air view of Potholes Reservoir

Carp spawning

Mesa and tributary of Crab Creek

Turtles

Meadow salsify

Cinnamon teal

34 Lower Potholes Area
Columbia National Wildlife Refuge and Lava and Goose Lakes Wildlife Recreation Areas

Best season: Winter, spring, summer
Highlights: Waterbirds, shorebirds, songbirds, small mammals; scenery
Camping: Yes
Contact: Refuge Mgr., Columbia National Wildlife Refuge, P.O. Drawer F, Othello, 99344. 509-488-3831

Jewel-like blue lakes set in buttes and mesas of pinkish lava, with fringes of white-barked aspen and a background of gray-green sage, make this one of Washington's most beautiful areas—a sort of paradise on a small scale in the vast Central Washington desert.

To reach the wildlife area from the west, take the Dodson Road exit from Interstate Highway 90 and drive south to O'Sullivan Road, then east on O'Sullivan past Potholes State Park. From here to Lava Lakes Road, just past where O'Sullivan Road turns north, any road headed south will take you to some fascinating part of the wildlife area. On a first visit, take the road marked with a refuge sign, just east of O'Sullivan Dam. Folders there will take you on a self-guided auto tour that can be made in less than an hour.

This is a place to explore by car for a few hours of a day. Then camp for several more days. You can take short, easy hikes to viewpoints on the high bluffs, or to smaller lakes choked with white Water-crowfoot buttercup. There are several designated campgrounds in the north part of the wildlife refuge.

The area is fascinating any time of year, although it is best avoided in hunting season. The larger lakes may be most interesting in winter, when lakes like Royal may be crowded with as many as 30,000 ducks and geese. Here as in other Central Washington wetlands, spring and fall bring hordes of ducks, geese, and shorebirds. You have a chance of seeing the rare sandhill crane, the magnificent bird that once "danced" its courtship on prairies across the nation.

But unlike many desert areas, this one still throbs with life in midsummer. Noisy Red-winged or Yellow-headed blackbirds "mob" an American kestrel, or perhaps even a rare Peregrine or Prairie falcon. The aggressive blackbirds wheel, dive and scream until he retreats. Nesting Mallards, Blue-winged, and grave-looking dark-red Cinnamon teal lurk in the reeds. Cliff swallows, always contentious, fight for mud houses on the rock. Killdeer complain. The activity goes on around the clock.

Basalt cliffs

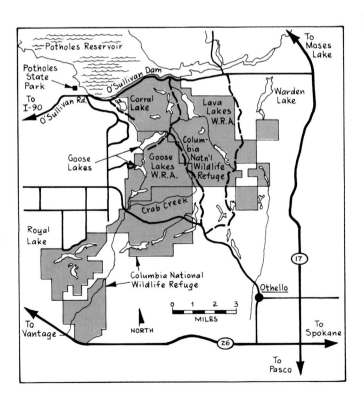

Red-winged blackbird's nest

Female Red-wing sitting on nest

Whistling swans on a small lake

Same nest ten days later

Killdeer

Pintail

35 Crab Creek
Wildlife Recreation Area

Best season: Spring
Highlights: Waterbirds, shorebirds; dunes
Camping: Undeveloped
Contact: Wash. St. Game Dept., Regional Office, P.O. Box 1237, Ephrata, 98823. 509-754-4624

Crab Creek W.R.A.'s 17,500 acres stretch along the floor of one of the cliff-walled coulees cut by Ice Age floods in the lava basin of East Central Washington. Canoe the creek—once an Indian route across the desert. Explore some of Washington's few sand dunes. Fish in rock-rimmed Lake Lenice. Discover the life of lazy marshes and barren cliffs.

To reach Crab Creek W.R.A. from the west, turn off State Highway 243 at Beverly onto the Smyrna Road and drive two miles. From the east, turn south onto the Smyrna Road from State Highway 26 at Royal City and drive 5 miles. The partly dirt, but good road runs the length of the W.R.A. Short walks take you to the reservoir, dunes, creek, marshes, or canyon wall.

There are parking areas and toilets, but no drinking water or other camping facilities.

Spring and early summer are the best times for a visit, as they are almost anywhere in the desert. The creek between the bridge in the W.R.A. and its mouth at the Columbia is then a fast but fairly easy canoe trip of about 5.5 miles (Scout it first to spot the one tight S-turn that must be portaged.) The sand dunes at the W.R.A.'s west end are abloom with their characteristic flowers, but they are no place for wildlife watching: The dunes are set aside for all-terrain vehicles and any animal you spot is likely to be scared off by a motor. Lake Lenice and the other lakes north of the creek are busy with fishermen. Steep rocky shores discourage most bird life.

Go to the coulee cliffs; or to the shallow, marshy parts of the creek where shore and water birds find food and shelter.

A canyon wren's cascading laugh floats down from the coulee's talus toe of broken rock. Cliff swallows dart near their mud nests. Mourning doves fly in pairs, hooting softly. And a pair of red-tailed hawks that have nested on one of the lava pillars scream keee-rrr as they circle in search of unwary ground squirrels. You will find the same hunters and hunted on many of the lava walls of this desert region.

In the marsh are noisy Red-winged and Yellow-headed blackbirds; dignified Canada geese; avocets feeding delicately on their stilt-like legs; Wilson phalaropes and a collection of other shore,

Abandoned farmhouse

swamp, and water birds. You may see a coyote hunting, placing each foot carefully, golden tail high, looking alert but relaxed. He hears or smells something in the tall shore grass, gives a short pounce with front paws and jaws coming together, and comes up shaking a bird in his jaws. He goes higher on the bank to eat. Birds that had taken alarm come back to their nests where he made his kill. Marsh life goes on.

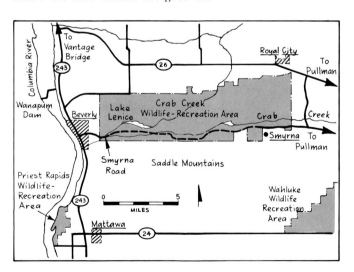

Killdeer on well-camouflaged nest

Killdeer eggs, camouflaged to look like rocks

36 Saddle Mountains
Saddle Mountains National Wildlife Refuge and Wahluke Slope Wildlife Recreation Area

Best season: Spring
Highlights: Desert life; views
Camping: No
Contact: Wash. St. Game Dept., Regional Office, P.O. Box 1237, Ephrata, 98823. 509-754-4624

Stop here someday to enjoy the wildlife of desert and lakes, the peaceful emptiness of sage and great space. Spring and early summer are the best times: the land is in bloom, small desert mammals are still active, and shorebirds and waterbirds are nesting on White Bluffs Lake.

Saddle Mountain National Wildlife Refuge is closed to the public. Adjacent 57,839-acre Wahluke Slope Wildlife Recreation Area is open only from sunrise to sunset, with no camping allowed. It is part of the Hanford nuclear-energy reservation closed back in World War II as part of the top-secret project of learning the secrets of the atom. Only recently was the public allowed here at all.

You can reach Wahluke Slope W.R.A. by driving south and west from Othello on State Highway 24; east from Yakima on 24 or northwest from Richland on 240, crossing the Vernita Toll Bridge over the Columbia; or south along the Columbia on State Highway 243. (This route takes you past a 2,051-acre satellite W.R.A. on the Columbia, deserted-looking in late summer but busy with nesting Canada geese in spring.)

W.R.A. signs on both sides of State Highway 24 mark the two entrances to Wahluke Slope W.R.A. The paved road that runs north from the highway climbs to the top of low Saddle Mountains. You can look across farm and desert to the Columbia's canyon and the whole of the Cascades on one side; and to wandering Crab Creek and even, on a very clear day, the hazy Blue Mountains on the other.

A dirt road runs along the ridge to its highest spot, 2,800-foot Wahatis Peak. But the view is not much better, and the last half mile is rough for an ordinary car.

The road that runs south from Highway 24 is the pre-war highway that led to the old White Bluffs ferry on the Columbia. Stop and walk a few yards to marshy White Bluffs Lake to watch Great blue herons winging slowly above the sage; families of big, low-flying Marsh hawks hunting together in early summer. A westward branch of the paved road leads down to the old ferry landing. In spring look for terns and gulls here. In winter, Bald and Golden eagles perch in trees along the banks and feed on the salmon that spawn and die in this last free-flowing stretch of the Columbia.

Columbia River below old Vernita ferry

If you go straight on the old highway, you will find the road barred at the edge of the bluffs above the river. But you can walk farther. Watch a shrike hunting insects in the sage like a miniature hawk with hooked beak. In the later afternoon, you can listen to the coyotes yip and howl and look across the golden river to science-fiction-like Hanford Atomic Works with the desert and mountains beyond.

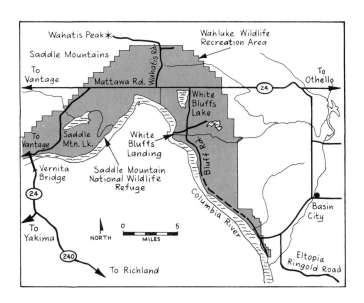

Yakima River from Rattlesnake Hills

37 Rattlesnake Slope Wildlife Recreation Area

Best season: Spring
Highlights: Desert Life
Camping: Undeveloped
Contact: Wash. St. Game Dept., Regional Office, P.O. Box 1237, Ephrata, 98823. 509-754-4624

Rattlesnake

This 3,341 acres of sage and grassland, rolling from the Yakima River to the crest of the gently sculpted Rattlesnake Hills, has a barren beauty all its own. Almost "virgin" desert, locked up as part of the Hanford Atomic Energy Reservation until recently, it is a place to get to know some of the desert animals that are being driven from their homes as more and more of Eastern Washington becomes farmland.

To get there, follow Division Street north from Benton City or turn off State Highway 240 about five miles northwest of Richland onto the Benton City-Horn Rapids Road. About seven miles from Benton City or 11 from the 240 junction, a W.R.A. sign marks the lone jeep road that runs from the river up into the game area's hills.

There are no camping or other facilities. Bring your own water. Wear boots and watch your step: The Rattlesnake Hills are well named.

Spring, roughly April through June, is the time for a visit here. The desert crams most of its life into a few short months between winter cold and summer drought.

In this short season, the gray sage land suddenly is bright with blooms—many of them "ephemerals" like Bitterroot that send out hasty spring blooms and leaves, and then wither to spend summer and winter underground as fleshy roots.

The wildlife here is not unlike the plants. Some of the mammals will spend the winter in hibernation and the summer in aestivation, a summer sleep. These include the little gray Least chipmunk that scurries away to his burrow; the fat Yellow-bellied marmots that lumber about their rockpile colonies like little bears; and the Townsend's and other ground squirrels with their colonial burrows.

Animals as well as plants tend to be grayish here: The color probably reflects desert heat and helps camouflage animals.

Desert plants that do not wither usually have adaptations to conserve water—like tiny, tough-skinned, or light-colored leaves. Desert animals have special adaptations, too. The Sagebrush mouse and the Townsend's ground squirrel do not need water to drink. They metabolize their own from dry desert plants they eat.

Many desert animals spend their days in cool burrows and come out to feed only at night. Among them are little-known animals like the Northern grasshopper mouse, a tiny but fierce insect-hunter; and the Pygmy rabbit, Washington's only native burrowing rabbit. Look for the tracks of these night creatures as you seldom see the animals themselves.

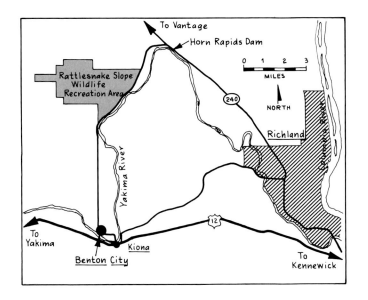

107

38 Toppenish National Wildlife Refuge

Best season: Early fall, late winter, spring
Highlights: Ducks, Canada geese
Camping: No
Contact: Refuge Mgr., Route 1, Box 1300, Toppenish, 98948. 509-865-2405

Like nearby Sunnyside W.R.A., this refuge is scattered wetlands and feeding fields for waterfowl. Scenery is not spectacular. Camping is forbidden. Much of the refuge is closed to the public from Mid-October to mid-January and hiking in the marshy parts of the rest is a chore.

Still, Toppenish Refuge is worth a detour winter or spring to see one of the densest concentrations of ducks, especially Mallards, in the world.

One part of the refuge lies just off State Highway 97, the Satus Pass Highway. Just over three miles south of Toppenish, turn east onto a gravel road just after the highway crosses a large drainage channel. Drive ¼ mile east and then ½ mile south to a bridge, and from your car enjoy flocks of ducks and geese in the wetlands along Toppenish Creek. Others can be seen from the highway where it crosses Toppenish Creek, about 1½ miles past the drainage channel.

Just past the creek crossing, a refuge sign on the right directs you to a signboard where refuge maps are available, headquarters where you can get more information, and to Pumphouse Road. You can drive gravel Pumphouse Road 11 miles, turn right at the pumphouse and pipe, and about a mile to the north find yourself at refuge wetlands along Toppenish Creek again. You can make a loop of about 15 miles roughly around this segment of the refuge by going north on Harrah, west on Yost, south on Island, and east again on Pumphouse Road.

The most interesting animal watching is in the wetlands near the creek. You may see the "powder puff" white undertail of a Nuttall's cottontail rabbit as he dashes away. Muskrats leave their silver wakes on the ponds. The lowly muskrat has his "use" in places like this: He keeps channels in the reeds open for the birds, and some, like Canada geese, build nests on his mounded grass houses.

You will see Red-tailed and Marsh hawks, and possibly a Bald eagle, in winter. The ducks, too, are most numerous then.

But spring brings songbirds, migrant shorebirds, and the mating rituals of the waterfowl. A female Mallard, swimming with her chosen mate of the year, tosses her head over her shoulder in ritual "defiance" of a rival suitor that actually serves to entice other males to their ritual. Groups of them gather, bow or arch their supple backs and display their irridescent green headfathers, and whistle.

Short-eared owl

Wild Iris

Sometimes it ends with a wild chase of the female on the wing. Such rituals seem designed to display the males' most striking features. And they seem to function to get all the birds "in the mood" for mating at the right time.

Other ducks have similar showy, rather comic courtships. Male pintails hold their pointed tails erect and mew. Buffleheads bob their heads, males showing their crests; Goldeneyes throw their decorated heads back.

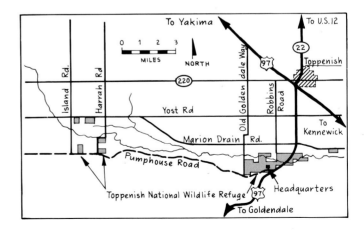

Great blue heron rookery

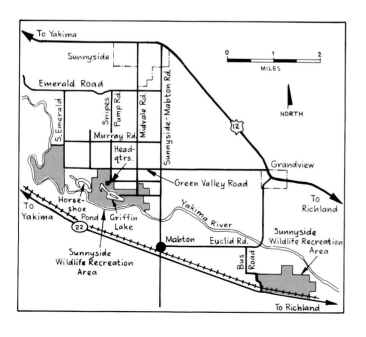

39 Sunnyside Wildlife Recreation Area

Best season: Spring
Highlights: Waterbirds, shorebirds
Camping: No
Contact: Wash. St. Game Dept., Regional Office, 2802 Naches Highway, Yakima, 98902. 509-248-5832

Ponds and willow swamps, sage and scablands make a quiet though unspectacular resting and nesting place for birds along the Yakima River.

Sunnyside W.R.A. is in three segments near the town of Mabton, 36 miles southeast of Yakima on State Highway 22. One portion is just off the highway. A turn north onto Bus Road five miles southeast of Mabton or onto the unnamed dirt road a mile further on takes you to parking areas. You can wander on foot from there. But part of this segment is a wildlife sanctuary closed to the public.

To reach the Sunnyside segments along the Yakima River, take the Mabton-Sunnyside Road north from Mabton. At two miles, a turn west onto McGee Road takes you to Griffin Lake, with good watching from your car when it is not busy with hunters or fishermen. From McGee Road, a right onto Midvale and a left onto Holaday will skirt the segment and take you to a parking area near headquarters. You can walk to more water- and swampbird watching. From this headquarters area at the end of Holaday, a series of zig-zags of about a mile each will take you to the westernmost segment of the W.R.A. Drive north on Snipes Pump Road, east on Green Valley, north on Wendell Phillips, east again on Murray. Turn south on South Emerald and you will be driving along the W.R.A. boundary.

From the parking lot a mile south on South Emerald, you can hike west into the far end of the tight horseshoe bend in the river, and watch Great blue herons nesting in cottonwoods across the river. (Good binoculars or a telescope are essential.) The stilt-legged birds with snaky necks and spear-like beaks are a familiar sight stalking in shallow waters, usually alone. It is somehow incongruous to see them crowded together in trees, on the big bundles of sticks that are their nests. (In fact, though, they often sit in trees and preen, using their beaks to take a powder that crumbles from special down on their chests and rub it through their feather like dry shampoo.)

Do not go near the rookery. Young herons are easily frightened and may fall to their deaths. Besides, heron nesting spots are not entirely pleasant places: The ground often is white with excrement, the air filled with the yipping of the young and the smell of rotten frogs and fish.

Sunnyside W.R.A. is a day-use area only, with no camping facilities. Spring and early summer are the best times for a visit.

110

Ring-necked pheasant

40 McNary Area

McNary National Wildlife Refuge and McNary Wildlife Recreation Area

Best season: Winter, spring
Highlights: Ducks and geese, Burrowing owls, desert mammals
Camping: Nearby parks
Contact: Refuge Mgr., McNary Natl. Wildlife Refuge, Box 308, Burbank, 99323. 509-547-4942

Stretches of sage and farm fields just outside the Tri-Cities, along the dammed Columbia and Snake Rivers, come alive with birds from September through May. Year 'round, they are a haven for some of the odd creatures of the desert.

The major parts of both McNary National Wildlife Refuge and McNary Wildlife Recreation Area flank State Highway 395 about seven miles southeast of Pasco. A refuge sign directs you to McNary National Wildlife headquarters. The state area is almost just across the road: Gravel roads south of Burbank take you down to sloughs, sage and willows along the river.

These are areas to visit for a few hours or a day. The national refuge bars camping and the W.R.A. has no facilities. (You can camp in Hood Park just east of Burbank.) There is little space for hiking. Most of McNary Wildlife Refuge is closed to the public. (There is good birdwatching of some of the ponds from the "blind" of your car, though, and you can walk along the pond near headquarters.)

Winter after hunting season, when Canada geese and ducks number in the thousands, and spring when shorebirds and waterbirds are moving through and settling in to nest, are the times for a visit.

As suburbs and farming have spread around the Tri-Cities area, these wildlife lands have become more important as a refuge for desert animals. You can see the effects of civilization at McNary Refuge: Nesting boxes for Canada geese are built on stilts over the ponds to keep the birds safe from marauding dogs.

Animals forced out of their desert homes by farms have been concentrated at McNary. In the sandier stretches are two little-known and seldom-seen desert mammals: Ord's kangaroo rats hop about at night, gathering seeds to store in networks of underground tunnels. The little grayish, tan-tailed Pygmy rabbit digs burrow networks and comes out from dusk to dawn to nibble greens.

Keep an eye on fence posts for a small owl without "ear" tufts, bobbing nervously on long, unfeathered legs. This Burrowing owl is a daytime hunter who usually nests in old ground squirrel holes that have been enlarged by badgers—who probably ate the ground squirrels. The owls have

Short-eared owl

Killdeer

grown rare as they lost desert habitat to farms. A biologist tried for years to encourage them at McNary by digging holes for them, with little success. Then farming forced more badgers into McNary. They dug the holes, and the owls increased.

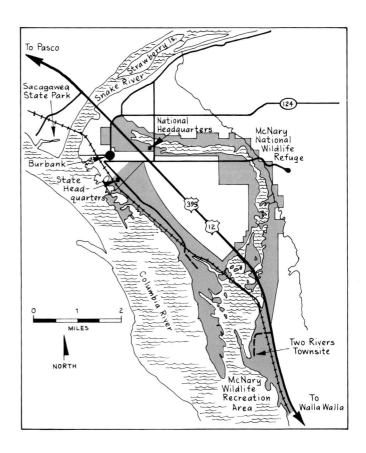

113

Burrowing owl

Sea gull attacking a live carp

41 Umatilla
National Wildlife Refuge

Best season: Early fall, winter, spring
Highlights: Waterbirds, shorebirds
Camping: No
Contact: Refuge Mgr., Box 239, Umatilla, Oregon, 97882. 503-922-3232

After you leave the drama of the Columbia Gorge through the Cascades, heading east, there is a new drama waiting for you in the thousands of water-fowl migrating or wintering on the river's "desert islands" and sage-edged sloughs.

Umatilla National Wildlife Refuge is one of the best places to get the feel of the huge flocks of ducks and geese that move north and south across the continent each year. The refuge stretches more than 20 miles along both sides of Lake Umatilla, the reservoir backed up behind John Day Dam on the Columbia. If you are coming from the west, on State Highway 14, look for refuge signs and Crow Butte Road, which takes you to a rocky river island with a picnic area, beach, camping and prime waterbird watching. Shooting is restricted, so this is a good place to come in fall hunting season. If you are coming from the north, State Highway 221 runs south from Prosser to the refuge. From the northeast, drive west on Highway 14 and look for refuge signs. Or, at Plymouth, take a right toward some mobile homes instead of a left just before you get on the bridge to Oregon. Follow the road north along the river to Patterson Slough.

The best animal-watching spots in the refuge probably are Patterson Slough, with its beavers, swamps full of shorebirds in spring, and snags where eagles rest; Whitcomb Island, marked by signs about 10 miles west of the Highway 221 junction (Long-billed curlews nest in the grass here); and Crow Butte.

Camping is not allowed in the refuge. Hiking is limited, but you can take interesting walks in the Patterson Slough area, on Crow Butte and Whitcomb Islands, and just along the river. Midday in late winter or spring is the best time for a visit, when the wintering or migrating ducks and geese are resting in the quiet waters between shore and islands or on sandbars. At dawn and dusk, and especially on moonlit nights, they may be away feeding in the farmer' fields: Their early morning and late afternoon feeding flights are a dramatic sight.

Counts have found 100,000 Canada geese and almost 200,000 mallards on the refuge in midwinter. These species are not newcomers to the area. Canada geese and ducks rested and nested on 26 Columbia River islands drowned when John Day Dam was built. The refuge exists largely to mitigate for the loss of this wildfowl habitat. But irrigation, by replacing sagebrush with grain and sprouts of winter wheat, has provided the wintering

Western meadowlark

birds with more food and probably increased their number far beyond the number that stayed when the land was "wild."

This causes wildlife managers some worry: Disease can spread quickly through crowds of birds like those at Umatilla and the birds can damage crops, although so far refuge managers have only heard scattered complaints.

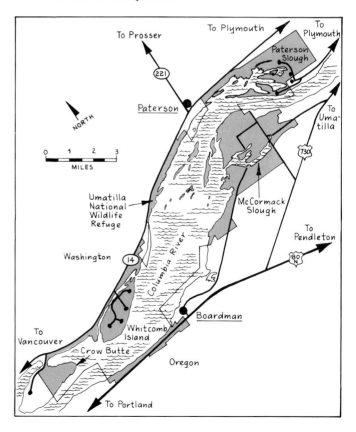

115

Sherman Creek

42 Roosevelt Lake
Coulee Dam National Recreation Area and Sherman Creek Wildlife Recreation Area

Best season: Spring
Highlights: Ospreys, songbirds; lake scenery
Camping: Yes
Contact: Wash. St. Game Dept., Regional Office, North 8702 Division Street, Spokane, 99218. 509-456-4082

Coulee Dam National Recreation Area, stretched along the 150-mile-long reservoir behind Grand Coulee Dam; and adjacent 8,068-acre Sherman Creek Wildlife Recreation Area, take you from desert sage and rimrock up to mountain forests of pine and larch, and from the edge of the coulee-scarred Columbia Plateau to the Okanogan Highlands that roll across the northeast edge of the state.

Developed campgrounds are scattered along the reservoir, particularly on the south and east sides. You can camp in Sherman Creek W.R.A. but there are no particularly good spots for it. Spring comes late to this north country: May and June usually are the best months for the abundant wildflowers and songbirds of desert and open pine forest.

The rimrock and mountains along this now-dammed stretch of the Columbia have a colorful history. A Hudsons Bay fur-trading post, Fort Colville, stood where the Colville enters the Columbia from 1826 to 1871. The U.S. Army built Fort Spokane at the Spokane-Columbia confluence in 1881, to keep an eye on the Indians after the Chief Joseph War. The area had its gold rush, and was once known for its outlaws: the Fruitland area was called Robbers' Roost for its rustlers. At Creston, a famous outlaw, Harry Tracy, shot himself to avoid being taken by a posse. And the building of 550-foot-high Grand Coulee Dam in the 1930s became an instant bit of legend.

The trip will show you a range of species from desert birds and burrowers of the Columbia Basin to waterbirds on the reservoir and mountain species—like the Northern three-toed woodpecker and Mountain chickade—in higher parts of Sherman Creek W.R.A., reached by turning north from Highway 20. The mammals here are the interesting mixture of Cascade and Rocky Mountain types described in the section on the Pend Oreille W.R.A.

Look for ospreys, particularly along the Sanpoil near Keller. The hawk's whistles rise higher and higher; then he plummets suddenly to the water and splashes up with a fish. Look for an American kestrel crying shrilly and flycatching from a snag. Despite its common name of Sparrow hawk, it eats more insects than birds.

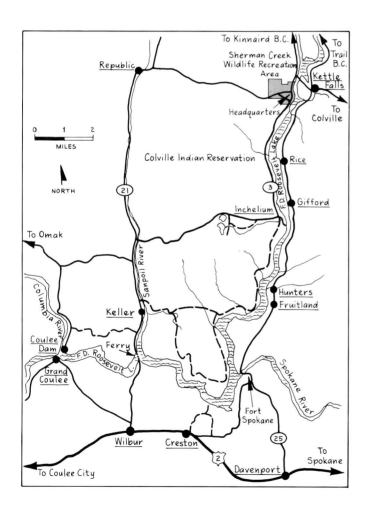

Osprey along the Sanpoil River

Abandoned log barn

43 Pend Oreille Area
Little Pend Oreille and LeClerc Creek Wildlife Recreation Areas

Best season: Spring
Highlights: White-tailed deer, songbirds
Camping: Yes
Contact: Wash. St. Game Dept., Regional Office, North 8702 Division Street, Spokane, 99218. 509-456-4082

The gently rolling pine forests in the state's northeast corner offer you spring wildflowers, fall mushroom hunting, winter snowshoeing or cross-country skiing, and—any time of year—an introduction to Rocky Mountain wildlife types whose range barely laps into Washington.

Leclerc Creek W.R.A. so far is only the germ of a deer-and-fishing area that the state hopes will grow. It is a few small tracts scattered along the Pend Oreille River Valley, with good birdwatching for species of evergreens, waterside brush and deciduous trees, and open meadows. Drive north from Cusick or south from Ione on State Highway 31, or take the quieter, slower road along the east side of the river. Look for the small Game Department signs that mark wildlife lands and access to the river.

Camping is allowed but undeveloped. This is a good stop in your way to the Salmo Mountains to the north, a bit of wilderness that holds Washington's only moose and caribou.

Little Pend Oreille W.R.A., 40,861 acres, is one of the state's largest, busiest, and most developed game areas. Take State Highway 20 (294 on some maps) east from Colville, turn south on the road to Arden, go left or east at the four-way intersection, and follow the signs to W.R.A. headquarters. Or continue east, stopping at Crystal Falls beside the highway, and take one of the dirt roads that branch into the W.R.A. about three miles past the falls.

Exploring Little Pend Oreille W.R.A. by car is easy. The area has a network of more than 100 miles of good, clearly signed roads. Some continue on to the higher mountains of the Colville National Forest. There are several developed—and often crowded—campgrounds.

Go to Bayley or McDowell Lakes at dawn. Watch the Columbian ground squirrels nibbling in the meadows, a Great blue heron fishing, a muskrat making a silver V across the water. Take short hikes along the creeks or up the sunny hills, enjoying songbirds and drumming grouse. Drive the Blacktail Mountain Road up to a view over fold after fold of dark green mountains.

The area has some disadvantages for wildlife watching. It is so popular that other visitors may disturb you and the animals. Its miles of fairly dense pine forests may give you only a glimpse of deer. But it is a place to get to know the distinctive animal life of the east end of the state.

Pend Oreille River

The deer that bounds away with a "rocking-horse" gait, waving a white flag of a tail, is a White-tailed deer. White-tails, the Red squirrels that trill and scold you from the pines, and the Columbian ground squirrels of the meadows, are Rocky Mountain species whose range stretches to these Eastern highlands in Washington and across the Northeastern highlands to the Cascades. Other such eastern species found here are Red-tailed chipmunks on the higher peaks, and the scarce Western jumping mouse, a tiny mouse of meadows whose extremely long tail helps balance him as he hops about on his hind legs.

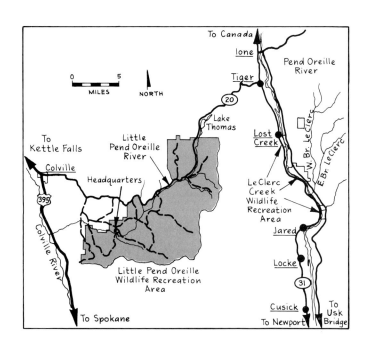

119

44 Turnbull National Wildlife Refuge

Best season: Any time
Highlights: Trumpeter swans, waterbirds
Camping: No
Contact: Refuge Mgr., Rt. 3, Box 107, Cheney, 99004. 509-234-4723

A visit to Turnbull National Wildlife Refuge's marshy ponds and meadows set among pines is the lazy man's way to get to know wildlife in this end of the state. And it is a must for any wildlife lover in the area. You can't camp; and most of the refuge is closed to the public, for the sake of the waterbirds that winter and breed here. But the refuge is closed to all hunting, making its variety of habitats an excellent place to watch birds and mammals any time of year. And Turnbull's self-guided nature tour, taken mostly by car with a few short, level walks, probably shows and tells you more about wildlife in an hour or two than you will learn anywhere else in Eastern Washington in several days.

To reach the refuge, drive south from Cheney four miles on the Cheney-Plaza Road, and turn east or left at the refuge sign. Pick up a free tour map and the folder that lists Turnbull's birds at the signboard near the entrance or at headquarters.

Fall migration, from September to December, brings the greatest number of waterbirds to the refuge. Spring migration, at its height in April and May, is sparser and shorter. But the birds are going through their courtship antics and the wildflower show is underway. June is the height of nesting season. And even in hot, still July and August you will see plenty of life, including species unusual in Washington.

Two unusual animals are among the first birds you are likely to see, on Winslow Pool near refuge headquarters. Turnbull has Washington's only nesting colony of the rare Trumpeter swans—magnificent white birds almost wiped out as civilization swept over their homes on prairie potholes. This colony was transplanted to rebuild the species.

Near the dignified swans, Black terns swoop and cry, hunting insects on the wing. Their nesting grounds barely reach into the east end of the state.

The tour offers a look at a beaver lodge (you may spot a mink or a muskrat, too) and a blind for watching waterbirds. Enjoy the comic posing of the fat little Ruddy ducks—especially during their awkwardly splashy courtships, when males fan

Trumpeter swan

Eastern kingbird

their tails, puff their chests, tuck their chins, and patter along the water before the beloved, uttering clucks and ticks. Watch the water ballet of Eared grebes, in which the birds rise on the water and circle around one another, necks almost entwined. Keep an eye out for coyotes and White-tailed deer. You don't have to look for Red squirrels and Yellow-pine chipmunks. They will scold you noisily.

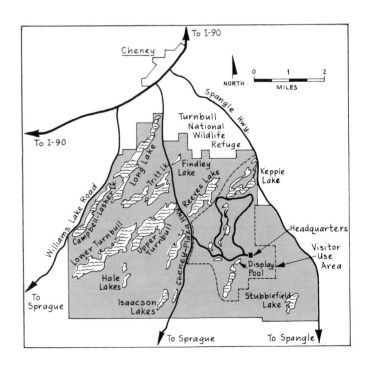

White-fronted goose

Snow goose

Trumpeter swans

Wild onion

Columbian ground squirrel

Keppler Lake

Bighorn sheep

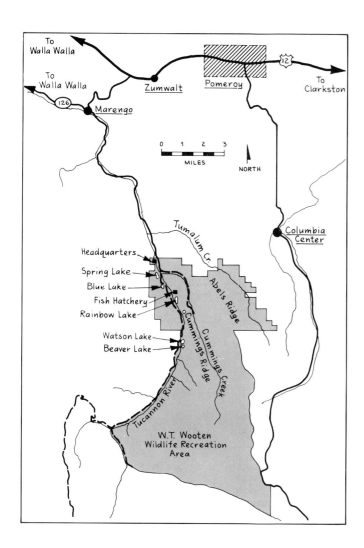

45 W.T. Wooten Wildlife Recreation Area

Best season: Spring
Highlights: Deer, Bighorn sheep, songbirds; wildflowers
Camping: Yes
Contact: Wash. St. Game Dept., Regional Office, North 8702 Division Street, Spokane 99218. 509-456-4082

This 11,185-acre state wildlife area is the perfect gateway to the Blue Mountains.

To get there, turn off State Highway 12 six miles east of Pomeroy, and drive four miles to Marengo. Signs saying W.T. Wooten direct you to the road up the Tucannon River. Follow it about 15 miles to the W.R.A., or farther into the Umatilla National Forest and the higher mountains.

In the game area, you can camp along the Tucannon River, enjoying wildflowers and eight nearby ponds in spring and summer, or the elk that venture into the valley bottom in winter. Or hike the open hills with an advantage you don't have in the nearby Umatilla National Forest: The state has banned off-road vehicles so you won't meet noisy motorcycles. (One warning, however: In this trailless rattlesnake country, carry water, a map, compass, and a snakebite kit, and watch your step.)

The best time for seeing elk is mid-December to Mid-March, when deep winter snows often bring them down to forage in the valley bottom, near the main road along the Tucannon. You can make this a stop on your way to snowshoe or cross-country ski in the higher national-forest land.

Almost any time of year, you have a chance of seeing the small herd of Bighorn sheep begun from transplants in 1960. Look for them on Cummings Ridge, east of the main road about a mile up the valley from headquarters. Or ask at headquarters or the fish hatchery where they have been seen lately.

Spring and summer, when the main road and the Tucannon are crowded with campers and fishermen, are the times to visit the W.R.A.'s back country. Take Cummings Creek Road through groves and meadows along the creek valley, or walk the open hillsides bright with wildflowers typical of the Blue Mountains—flaming Scarlet gilia; and Clarkia, its bright pink petals looking as if someone had torn them to shreds.

Like the W.R.A.s running down the East Cascades, this is a transition area between mountain conifer forest and dry bunchgrass country. Here as

Elk herd in spring

there, the wildlife watching is excellent, thanks to the open country and the variety of "niches"—conifers, streamside brush and deciduous trees, rocky areas, and near-desert bunchgrass. The birds and mammals you will see are much the same, except that there are hints of Idaho and Rocky Mountain species, as there are in the northeastern highlands of the state. You may see coyotes, badgers, chipmunks, ground squirrels, hawks, owls, songbirds, and game birds—including the introduced wild turkey, a thinner version of his descendant the domestic turkey, but with the same strutting, tail-fanning and chest-puffing habits carried on here in the thickets.

Bighorn sheep

Elk   *White-tailed deer*

Lupine

Brown-eyed Susan

Stonecrop

Tucannon River

Pictographs near mouth of the Grande Ronde River

46 Eastern Blue Mountains
Asotin Creek, Chief Joseph and Grouse Flats Wildlife Recreation Areas

Best season: Spring
Highlights: Deer, songbirds; scenery
Camping: Undeveloped
Contact: Wash. St. Game Dept., Regional Office, North 8702 Division Street, Spokane, 99218. 509-456-4082

The southeast corner of Washington manages to be spectacular yet somehow gentle. Here are the deep canyons of the Grande Ronde and the Snake, marked with Indian petroglyphs; high plateaus of wheat where you seem on a level with distant snow-capped mountains; and the Blue Mountains themselves, sensuous curving folds cut by harsh rock outcrops and sudden lights and darks where evergreen woods of moist, shady slopes change to the parched grass of drier ones.

Three state game areas—Asotin Creek, Grouse Flats, and Chief Joseph W.R.A.s—let you get to know the wildlife of the lower mountains. And if you have never seen this part of the state, getting there can be half the fun.

Asotin Creek W.R.A., 8,725 acres, is a journey into the Old West. From little Asotin with its old-fashioned storefronts go west on Bauermeister Road. About two miles outside of town take the right fork onto Asotin Creek Road and drive ten miles up the canyon, past weathered corrals and ranch buildings. A W.R.A. sign at another fork in the road tells you you have reached the game area. Either fork takes you about four miles up a beautiful canyon, bright with flowers in spring. Side roads show you views from ridges. You can camp here (there are no developed campgrounds) or continue into the Umatilla National Forest and the higher mountains for longer hikes and high-mountain animals.

To get to Chief Joseph W.R.A., drive south from Asotin along the Snake River canyon, and cross the Grande Ronde—a canyon just as dramatic, but very different, with its tight meanders. The W.R.A. is on both sides of the road just south of the Grande Ronde. A marked dirt road turning east takes you to headquarters. Only a jeep road and no developed trails reach into the area. Its dry, open country is perfect for short springtime backpacks up on the ridges looking over the rivers, and down to their canyon edges.

Grouse Flats, an elk calving ground on a foothill bench, is a rather uninteresting anticlimax after the long drive south from Asotin on State Highway 129, into Oregon and back again. But the drive is

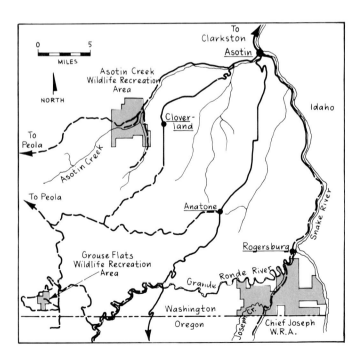

North Fork Asotin Creek

exciting: across a high wheatfield plateau where you feel on top of the world, and down into the twisting canyon of the Grande Ronde.

Springtime is the best season to visit any of these W.R.A.s, as this rain-shadowed side of the Blue Mountains is parched in late summer, noisy with hunters in fall, and rather drab in winter.

The wildlife is much like that of similar parts of the East Cascades, where pines dwindle into bunchgrass. But here there are overtones not only of the Rocky Mountains—as in the transplanted White-tailed deer—but also of Oregon wildlife, as in the Green-tailed towhees that sometimes wander here.

A PRIMER FOR WATCHING WILDLIFE

Why Watch Wildlife?

Most people probably picture wildlife watchers as little troops in tennis shoes, clutching guidebooks and peering eagerly through binoculars for a glimpse of the rare whatzit.

There is some truth to the image. Beginners often go in groups to learn. Others like company. And just as some people who love books become collectors or rare first editions, some wildlife enthusiasts become chiefly interested in spotting rare species.

But learning wild creatures' names and checking off the ones you have seen on a list barely begins the joy of getting to know wild animals.

Watching wildlife brings moments that are intense and profound: White Snow geese restless on the wintry tide flats for their spring journey north, rising in a swirling cloud with the high north wind in their voices, some starting the long flight to their nesting ground on the barrens of an ice-bound island north of Siberia.

There is comedy in wildlife: Fat baby ground squirrels tussling outside their burrows; the rivalry of chubby little black-and-white male Buffleheads for a drab female. One duck dives and firmly "gooses" the other suitor, who skitters off, splashing along the water.

Wild life has its parallels in our "civilization." There are parables in watching even the robins and starlings in your yard: The urging of the glands breaks up peaceful wintertime groupings. The conquest of territory and status comes before seeking of a mate.

As happens when you gain any kind of knowledge, watching wildlife makes your world fuller—of perceptions, meanings, and mystery.

After you watch wild birds and mammals awhile, you will be surprised how much you see and hear that you missed before. Even in the city, you are surrounded by a new world of activity, chatter, and song. Creatures glimpsed from the corner of your eye as you drive your car take on definite identities from a silhouetted profile or a manner of moving.

Once you know wildlife, a hike or a camping trip offers you much more than peace and pretty scenery. Even if you are not on the lookout for animals, you know what is around you when you hear the high, monotonous "tsk" of a Townsend's chipmunk scolding from the bushes; the nasal "enk" of an alarmed pika on an alpine rockpile. And they remind you that you are in a particular wild community.

This community has its own forms of "cooperation" and "competition." The tunnel with a hard-packed entrance mound you see in Eastern Washington may have been dug by a ground squirrel, enlarged by a badger that ate the squirrel, used by a Burrowing owl after the badger was gone—and shared by certain mice and insects at any of these stages.

This community has its own rituals of behavior, its own adaptations to the conditions around it, its own history. Getting to know wildlife teaches you to "see" all these.

Watching ducks on a lake in spring, you see much more than handsome, colorful birds. You know that the baleful black-and-white Goldeneyes, throwing their heads back grandly, are engaged in courtship.

You know that Mallards, Shovellers, Teal, and others called "puddle ducks" or "dabblers" have long, broad bills that serve them as shovellers and strainers in the shallows where they search for food. They have long necks to help them reach the bottom, and long wings that let them spring directly from the water in the reedy, confined ponds they frequent. In contrast, the fat, sleepy little Ruddy ducks and other divers well out on the water are built for easy maneuvering underwater. Bills and necks are short. But their legs, set well back for paddling, often make it hard for them to walk on land. And they often must patter a long way over the surface before their short wings carry them aloft.

You can "see" a bit of history in the lone male Wood duck in this assembly, striking in his particolored beak and plumage and drooping, irridescent green crest. In his gala attire he was sought for trout-fly material as well as for flesh. The species almost became extinct early in this Century. With years of protection, it made a strong recovery farther east. But it is still uncommon here.

Snowshoe hare at Colonial Creek, North Cascades National Park

Where Should You Go?

This book by no means covers all the good wildlife-watching areas in Washington. It covers the state's national parks and recreation areas, national wildlife refuges, and state wildlife-recreation areas. But animal watching may be just as good in mountaintop wilderness areas or big-city parks. Your local Audubon Society is a good source of information on wildlife-rich spots near your home. The Society keeps up on mammals as well as birds, and has chapters in most large cities. A good book for more specialized "birders" is "A Guide to Bird Finding in Washington," by Terence R. Wahl and Dennis R. Paulson, published by the Whatcom Museum Press, Bellingham.

The areas described in this book do include most of the state's largest and best known wildlife-watching areas. And they offer you a cross-section of the state's many wildlife communities.

These communities and broad life zones in Washington vary somewhat from north to south, but much more from east to west.

In Southern Washington you can find a handful of animals more typical of California and Oregon: These include the Scrub and Pinon jays, the California ground squirrel, and the little Ord kangaroo rat that hops about the desert at night. A few northland animals, like the moose and the Woodland caribou, have ranges that extend barely into the north edge of the state.

But the Pacific Ocean on the west and the prevailing winds that blow from it to the east; the north-south barrier of the Cascades and other highlands, with their altitude changes and effects on rain and snowfall; mean that differences of terrain, climate, soil, water, food, supply, and hence also of animal life, are most strongly marked as you go east or west in Washington.

The Pacific shore at the extreme west is wet and stormy. But ocean waters keep from being very hot or very cold.

It is a place where you may glimpse the soaring birds of open ocean, like the albatross; or marine mammals like whales and sea lions. Its rock pinnacles are a haven where sea birds, awkward on land, raise their young in close-packed colonies safe from land marauders.

It is the major arterial for migrant shorebirds and waterbirds migrating west of the Cascades. Fewer, although still very large numbers, use the Puget Lowland where Puget Sound deadends short of the Lower Columbia.

Lowland Western Washington's sheltered bays, tideflats, estuaries, lakes, marshes, and sloughs are migration stops and winter resorts for many birds of water, shore, and marsh. They are breeding places for some.

Almost any place you go has its own distinctive and interesting community of songbirds. Western Washington offers many such groupings. Old ever-

Black oyster catcher, Olympic National Park Ocean Strip

green woods, brushy second-growth forests, open fields, and watersides each have their own distinctive collections of birds, too many to name.

From sea level to fairly high in the mountains you can find most typical Western Washington mammals, or their signs: muskrat, mink, otter, beaver, Mountain beaver, Snowshoe hare. Douglas squirrel, Townsend's chipmunk, Black-tailed deer, Black bear. As with birds, you must look in the right kinds of habitats to find them. Some are extremely particular: Western gray squirrels insist on oaks. Columbian white-tailed deer almost became extinct as farmers took over their brushy river bottoms.

Where the trees thin out at subalpine heights in the mountains, you begin to find a very different kind of bird and mammal community: One with special adaptations to life amid crags, cold, and snow. Here are shaggy white sure-footed mountain goats. Here are squeaking pikas, short-eared relatives of rabbits: Short extremities lessen loss of body heat in cold winters. Here are ptarmigan, that have feathered legs and turn white in winter; and Clark's nutcrackers that store seeds in fall, thus getting an early start on nesting when they return to their high meadows and groves in spring. The Douglas squirrels and Townsend's chipmunks of rainy lowland Western forests of red-trunked evergreens were dark brown, with rusty tones. Here at subalpine heights are the Golden-mantled ground squirrel and the very similar-looking Yellow-pine chipmunk. Their light coats and strong stripes probably help camouflage them in this open country of strong lights and shade.

Mountains wring the moisture out of air that cools as it rises to go over them. Air warms up as it descends again and rain is less likely to fall. Hence the increasing dryness as you go down the east side of the Cascades and into the desert of the low Columbia Basin beyond. The dry San Juan Islands in the lee of the Olympics and the prairie country near Centralia leeward of the Willapa Hills are miniature examples of this "rain shadow" effect. Both Western Washington areas have wild communities akin to those of dry Eastern Washington.

You see a new animal world as you reach the open pine forests on this dry East side of the Cascades. Some Western Washington mammals reappear: Mink, beaver, River otter, muskrat are found across the state, wherever they find the kinds of food and water they need. Some species change color: Bobcats, coyotes and Snowshoe hares west of the Cascades have rusty tones in their coats. On the east side they tend toward yellow or gray, colors that may reflect heat as well as camouflage them better. Some Western Washington species are not found at all from the pine forests eastwards, for example, the Mountain beavers, sole members of a primitive rodent family that burrow in moist brushy areas and come out at night to harvest greens and pile them in little haystacks. Townsend's chipmunks on the west are replaced by Yellow-pine chipmunks on the east. Two kinds of mole are largely replaced by Pocket gophers. New species appear, like Mountain or bighorn sheep. Porcupines, that seem to regard pine bark and buds as beefsteak but often shun the hemlock and fir of wetter forests, become more common.

There is a new community of songbirds on this dry side of the mountains. Their colorful plumage; the openness of the country; and the mixture of habitats in the foothills—woods, streamside brush, and open grass and sage—make for some of the best bird watching anywhere.

The Columbia Basin, that stretches east from the Cascades except in Northern Washington, was once a vast plain of basalt built up as this thin lava poured quietly from cracks in the ground, time after time. It is broken now by low hills, river canyons worn down through millions of years, and coulee channels cut suddenly by Ice Age floods, when glacial dams burst and sent massive lakes tumbling over the desert.

Coyote

Canada geese, Umatilla National Wildlife Refuge

You meet a new animal assembly here. Mammals are gray, like the desert. They burrow, protecting themselves from heat and drought in the cool underground. Many of them, like the Least chipmunk; the Yellow-bellied marmot; the Townsend's, Washington's, and Columbian ground squirrels, spend as much as two-thirds of the year asleep, hibernating through winter's cold, aestivating through summer's drought. Others, like the mice, rabbits, and Kangaroo rats, dodge the heat and dryness by carrying on their activities by night. The desert has a hunter to match its burrowers: the badger, a grizzled, gray-and-yellow member of the weasel family with powerful digging claws.

There are birds typical of the desert. The names of Sage sparrow, Sage grouse, Sage thrasher, Canyon wren tell you they belong here. The Western meadowlark, perhaps the most beautiful of singers, drops his liquid notes from sage tops. The magpie nests in waterside thickets and scavenges over the dry land. The hook-billed Loggerhead shrike impales his prey on desert twigs.

The marshes and lakes in the desert, some natural but most artificial or accidental products of irrigation, offer you the other side of life in the Columbia basin. This is another of the major arterials on the Pacific flyway for migrants. And it is a nesting area for many water, marsh, and shore birds, including some we normally think of in connection with salt water. There are nesting colonies of gulls and terns here.

Many of the species are familiar from lowland Western Washington: Marsh hawks, Great blue herons, Killdeer, Mallards, Canada geese. But many are different. Yellow-headed blackbirds join the Red-wings in honking and screaming at you from the rushes. Instead of strange shorebirds like the Black oystercatcher with his chisel-like orange bill prying oysters from rocks, here you find equally odd shorebirds like the delicate Avocets, with their stilt-like legs and sleek black, white, and pinkish plumage, probing in shallows with needle-like, up-curved bills.

The Okanogan Highlands that roll across the north edge of the state east of the Cascades have enough snow and rainfall to support evergreen forests. Toward the east end of the state, land begins to rise again. Rainfall increases, and pine forests replace desert. In the southeast corner of the state are the Blue Mountains.

Wildlife in these highlands is much like that of the East Cascades, with similar climate, terrain, and plant life. But Cascade species begin to be replaced by Rocky Mountain types. The squirrels are white-bellied Red squirrels instead of orange-bellied Douglas squirrels. White-tailed deer mingle with or replace the mule deer.

In deciding where to watch wildlife, you will want to consider what kind of accommodations an area has for you as well as what kind of wildlife it accommodates.

Although all the areas listed in the book are public lands, they offer the visitor very different kinds of welcomes.

The national parks offer the most spectacular scenery. They do the most for their visitors. They offer developed car-camping areas and well-tended trails for hikers. As they are wildlife sanctuaries where hunting is banned, some animals may not scatter and hide as much as they do in other areas. But for the best wildlife watching in national parks, come prepared to hike at least a few miles. The parks exist to protect spectacular scenery, not to hack roads through it. What roads there are are usually too busy and narrow for safe and easy wildlife watching.

The national wildlife refuges were set aside not for people but for animals. Most but not all of them exist mainly for the migratory waterfowl popular with hunters (whose money foots much of the bill for the refuges).

Most national wildlife refuges allow some hunting, and so are best avoided during hunting season: roughly mid-October through mid-January.

Most national wildlife refuges bar overnight camping. Many of them close much of their land to the public entirely. You should obey these restrictions. Even a "harmless" birdwatcher could frighten birds from sanctuary areas into the range of waiting gunners, or frighten nesting birds into

Canada geese

abandoning their nests or exposing them to enemies like gulls or coyotes.

Compensating for these shortcomings, national wildlife refuges do offer about the best "lazy-man's" wildlife watching available. These areas have been chosen because they harbor large numbers of animals. Much can be seen from cars or on short, level walks of less than a mile. Some, like Turnbull, Ridgefield, and Columbia, have excellent self-guided tours that teach you a great deal in an hour or so.

State wildlife recreation areas, too, exist mainly for the animals and for the hunters and fishermen whose licenses helped pay for the land. The largest W.R.A.s' main purpose is to give deer and elk a home when they migrate down from snowy mountains in winter, thus protecting both the animals and the farms and ranches they would otherwise invade.

W.R.A.s, too, allow hunting and so are best avoided during hunting season. Most allow camping. But go expecting few or no maps or signs; rough, narrow roads that may be impassable; and no facilities. (There may be an outhouse. But bring your own water.)

The W.R.A.'s advantage often is the solitude they offer. They are little known and little used by anyone but hunters and fishermen. In their "off" seasons you often can roam their roads or take short hikes with the feeling that the area belongs to you and the wildlife.

Directions given in this book are seldom detailed. Much of the fun of watching wildlife is exploring and discovering on your own. And although wild animals are amazingly predictable in some ways—Why do Whistling swans return to particular fields near the Skagit each year, instead of similar fields nearby?—it usually is impossible to know just where the best wildlife watching will be.

Snowy owl near the Skagit Wildlife Recreation Area

When Should You Go?

There is no one best season for watching birds or mammals. Each change of the calendar introduces you to a new aspect of the wild world.

Spring may be the most exciting time. Waves of migrant birds pour into an area and hurry on. Some settle in to nest. They sing, stake out territories, carry on their amusing or impressive courtship rituals. (The singing and courtship also make spring a good time to begin to learn birds' names, as they keep the bird in one conspicuous place, where he usually makes noise that draws your attention, for some time.)

Wildflowers add to the gaiety. Ground squirrels, chipmunks, marmots, bears come out of winter sleep and stuff and sun themselves.

April and May are the peak of this activity in most of the state. But seasons merge into one another. Black brant, the little black sea geese with white clerical collars, may begin moving north along the mild ocean coast in late January. And spring in the high mountains may not come until August.

In late spring and early summer—June and July in most of the state—bird courtship and singing begin to taper off, and bushes and trees in full leaf hide more animal life from view.

There are compensations, though. The weather is warmer. Dirt roads generally are dried out. There still are lots of flowers. And animals' young are out and about: Spotted fawns come out of hiding and follow their mothers. Young tree squirrels nose cautiously about their home trees. Ground squirrels tussle near their burrows, scampering to safety at an adult's warning whistle. You can watch Marsh hawk families hunting together and sharing kills; and Belted kingfishers teaching their offspring to fish—The parent plummets to the water and catches a fish, comes back to his (or her) perch, and drops the fish again for the youngster to catch.

A strange quiet seems to settle over the world of wildlife in late summer heat. Most birds stop singing, their period of defending an exclusive territory over. Ducks and geese seem to vanish: This is their "eclipse," when they lose their strong wing and tail feathers and grow new ones in preparation for their long fall journey. While the molt goes on, they are unable to fly. Males take on the dull camouflaging of females, and skulk among reeds.

Seabirds leave their noisy nesting colonies and scatter again. The desert country subsides into its gray summer sleep. All but a few flowers wither and leave the land to sage and parched grass. Mammals like Yellow-bellied marmots, ground squirrels, Least chipmunks follow the fleshy-rooted ephemeral plants like bitterroot underground, as the animals go into aestivation.

This is the time to go to the high country, now hurrying its compressed spring, summer and fall between late snowmelt and early snowfall. Alpine and subalpine meadows rush through several changes of flower dress into the red and gold of frosted leaves. You can get to know the high-country animals and the animals that migrate here after spending winter and spring in the lowlands—deer, elk, many songbirds, and other birds from the soaring Golden eagles to the scurrying flocks of Blue grouse. Migration is not just a north-south flow. Animals also move from high to low, east to west—as gulls winging their way ocean-ward from desert nesting grounds show—and in a few instances north in winter, south in summer.

Already in August there are signs of fall. Berries ripen. The first migrant birds make their way south while others are still raising second broods (or first ones, as in the case of the state's official bird, the late-nesting American goldfinch that sings like a canary and skips up and down as it flies.)

Animals begin to put on weight or store food for the coming winter. By September, evergreen woods that seemed lifeless and silent in summer are noisy with scolding chipmunks. Tree squirrels challenge you and each other with high trills as they cut and cache cones. (These underground squirrel stores, sometimes hundreds of cones buried in mud, are where professional foresters get some of the seed that plants new forests.)

136

Pikas in alpine meadows, and Mountain beaver in lowland brush, cut greens and dry them in little haystacks to be stored. Beavers pile up underwater stores of brush and bark that you can spot by looking for twigs and branches projecting from the water. Chipmunks, marmots, bears, and other animals that sleep through the winter now spend most of their time gorging to put on fat.

Fall is mating season for many mammals. Elk in rut "bugle" in the mountains. (The sound is really more of a whistle ending in a grunt.) They are nice to hear, but watching is not advised. A bull elk in rut will attack bushes, trees, and you.

Fall bird migration is well underway in September. Terns, shorebirds, and more than a dozen kinds of seagull are moving through Puget Sound and along the ocean. Most swallows and many songbirds disappear to the south. Most of the migrant ducks seen now are the dabbling "puddle ducks." Divers, including loons and grebes, will appear later. Their southward movement continues through December. In general, fall migration seems more relaxed and leisurely than spring's hurried movement northward with its singing and courtship rituals.

October brings hunting season and thus ends prime fall wildlife-watching season in all but a few areas. (Places where no hunting is allowed include lakes in cities, national parks, and a few refuges like Turnbull.)

By the time hunting season ends in January, winter has prepared a new world for the wildlife watcher. If you ski or snowshoe in the high country you can see tracks of animals you seldom see in the flesh: weasels on their hunting circuits, shrews "swimming" through snow in their harried search for enough food to keep heat from draining from their tiny bodies. Nipped-off twigs near the big prints of the well-named Snowshoe hare are common. You might see the big prints of the lynx's pads that let him, too, "snowshoe" on the white soft blanket.

Many animals have changed color. Ptarmigan, White-tailed jackrabbits, and weasels and Snowshoe hares of high country have turned white. (Weasels and Snowshoe hares in low country stay brown.) Deer coats change from summer's reddish tan to winter's grayish buff, a help with camouflage.

By January, elk and deer usually have come down from the snowy highlands to winter ranges in the foothills. You can see them easily in the W.R.A.s along the East Cascades, especially Oak Creek, where elk are fed hay to keep them from invading and destroying farms and orchards.

Hawks, too, have gathered on lowland wildlife areas. Down from the North and the mountains are Bald and Golden eagles. Less noble than their looks, they scavenge the carcasses of spawned-out salmon along the state's rivers. You will see them on snags and bare limbs near the water.

Female red-winged blackbird

The wintering waterfowl settled in include Canada geese, Mallards, Pintails, Wigeons, Scaups, Scoters, Gadwalls, Goldeneyes, Shovelers, Ring-necked ducks, Ruddy ducks, Canvasbacks, three kinds each of teal and merganser, plus grebes, loons, and coots. They decorate lakes with a jewel-like variety of colors.

And there are the winter visitors with the snow on their plumage: swans, and thousands of Snow geese come from their barren breeding grounds on an island 90 miles north of Siberia to the Skagit flats. And every four to five years, apparently because of cyclic lemming-population crashes in their northern homes, big white Snowy owls invade open country and even cities in Washington in search of food.

The timing of all these animal events is only roughly predictable. In general, we can say that deer migrate down from the mountains in early winter, after their mating season and before heavy snows. But no one knows just when or why they will stream down the mountains by the hundreds. It may be that deer, like some people, feel the barometric changes "in their bones" and thus foretell storms. In mild winters, they may not come low at all.

We can say that a certain species of bird arrives roughly in March, or in May. But whether the main flocks arrive a few weeks early or late may depend

137

Black brant on Puget Sound

on weather and food supplies hundreds of miles back along their routes.

Thus, if you want to see a particular "event" on the animal calendar—say, elk gathered at Oak Creek; or black brant moving north along the ocean at Leadbetter Point—call the contact number listed in the guide before you make your trip. Ask what is happening this year.

Although there are no best seasons for wildlife watching, there are best hours. The best all-round time for watching birds and mammals is early morning, with late afternoon second. The activity of most daytime animals peaks in early morning and late afternoon. This is the time you are most likely to see them, as they move about, feed, court, or build homes. Dawn and dusk hours also give you a chance to get a glimpse of animals normally active at night, like muskrats and rabbits.

These morning and evening peaks are much more marked in the summer than in winter. In winter, animals often must spend nearly the whole of the short, frigid days busily seeking food in order to replenish their body heat and stay alive.

Waterbirds, shorebirds, and seabirds are another exception to the rule. They often are easiest to watch at midday, when they may be resting on the water or shore. At the Skagit Flats, Willapa Bay, and other places with broad tide flats, the state of the tide and the weather may be most important in determining whether the birds are close enough for you to see. A fairly high or incoming tide, and choppy waters, are likely to bring them close to shore.

Most nighttime animals, like beaver or flying squirrels, must be watched at night with the aid of a red flashlight (and skill and luck).

To really get to know wildlife, though, you should get to know the daily rhythms of some of your favorite places as well as their prime watching time. Some squirrel species are early risers. Others sleep late. Some birds, like swallows and robins, begin to twitter and carol well before dawn. Others are silent until hours after sunup. Some sing only at evening. Gulls may feed and squabble in the morning and loaf in the afternoon. These are clocks and rhythms you can get to know as well in your own yard or city parks as in wild areas.

How Do You Watch Animals?

Wildlife watching is a cheap pastime, as hobbies today go. All you need is a couple of guidebooks and a set of ordinary 7x35 binoculars. (More powerful binoculars are heavier and may tire the arms of an ordinary person. A bird-watcher's telescope with tripod magnifies much more. But it is awkward to lug on long hikes or to use in a hurry.)

I have always found that two guidebooks are much better than one for learning to identify anything—flowers, mushrooms, birds or mammals. Descriptions of color and sound, even colored drawings and photographs, vary greatly. If one book does not quite tally with what you saw and heard, check the other.

For birds, I recommend *Washington Birds, Their Location and Identification,* by Earl J. Larrison and Klaus G. Sonnenberg (published by the Seattle Audubon Society); plus the better illustrated *Birds of North America,* by Chandler S. Robbins *et al* (Golden Press, New York.)

For mammals, a good combination is Larrison's *Washington Mammals,* also published by the Seattle Audubon Society; plus Lloyd G. Ingles' *Mammals of the Pacific States* (Stanford University Press, 1965).

But field guides barely whet the appetite for information. Ingles' book goes well beyond identification into habits, habitats, and natural history. When you want to know more about birds, visit your local library and read the appropriate volume in Arthur Cleveland Bent's monumental though old-fashioned *Life Histories of North American Birds.* Among other excellent books are F.H. Kortright's *Ducks, Geese, and Swans of North America,* and Peter Matthiessen's poetic and informative *The Wind Birds,* on shore birds.

Like any hobby, wildlife watching takes time to learn. At first, you may find it frustratingly difficult even to find with binoculars what you saw with the naked eye. It takes time to learn to make a mental note of the features that identify a particular species. Identification is slow at first, when you must hunt through nearly all the possibilities in the guides and painstakingly try to match the exciting creature you saw with a dry description. Don't worry. It becomes much simpler as you learn the technique and can rule out many species you already know.

Here are some ways to speed up the learning:

—Go on outings with your local Audubon Society, or take classes or nature walks offered by many local parks departments and colleges.

—Go through your field guides over and over. Become familiar with names and pictures, with the areas and habitats where particular species are found, and with the order in which animals are listed. This order is the same in all good field guides.)

—Listen to records of bird songs and calls, and get to know the sounds made by birds and other vocal animals like squirrels and chipmunks. Voices can help you identify and save you time: If you know the up-and-down carol you hear is a robin, and a particular kind of chirp is an alarmed song sparrow, you don't have to waste time looking to see if the bird is a rare something-or-other.

—Go to museums, like the University of Washington's Burke Museum, that have stuffed specimens.

—Get to know the animals in captivity at the Olympic Game Farm at Sequim, a training spot for animals used in films; or, better, at Northwest Trek near Eatonville, a fascinating branch of the Tacoma zoo where native Northwest mammals are kept in habitats as close as possible to their natural ones. The enclosures are so realistic that the staff has a constant battle with the beavers to keep the creek flowing. This is a chance to get to know the kinds of habitats and behavior to look for in the wild, and to see things you could not see in "nature." For example, an underground passage has windows that look into small animals' dens.

It is much easier to get to know birds than to watch mammals. There simply are many more birds and kinds of birds than there are mammals. And birds spend a lot of time conveniently up in the air where we can see them, instead of in dens or underground tunnels. Birds are noisier, brigher, bolder. They can afford to be—They can take wing and fly away.

Because mammals are so much better camouflaged, and so many of them are active at night, getting to know them involves getting to know signs that they are around.

Learn to recognize tracks, droppings, the looks of different kinds of nests and burrows. At the desert edge of the Cascades, for example, you can easily tell the difference between Yellow-bellied marmot burrows in rock piles, tunnel complexes of ground squirrels with packed mounds of excavated earth at the entrances, and the much smaller chipmunk-den entrances, half hidden under a log or rock.

You can learn to see otter slides on slough banks, and the trails hares and other small animals make

Top to bottom: Badger, River otter and beaver at Northwest Trek

Water ouzel (dipper), Mt. Rainier National Park

through meadows and brush. Get down on your hands and knees and search thick grass for the labyrinth of "tunnels" mice have nipped and trampled through it. Follow the mazes to their nests. (The covered trails offer some protection. But the defense may not work against animals like coyotes and owls that hunt as much by sound as by sight.)

Get to know the difference between the volcano-like heaps of earth and the ridges pushed up by moles; and the workings of pocket gophers: mounds that usually have an off-center "plug" blocking the entrance, and cores of earth pushed out into snow and left when it melts in spring. Learn the difference between a bear's vertical scrapings when he wants sweet tree sap in spring, and a porcupine's tooth marks or bark rubbed off by elk antlers on a similar tree.

Beavers are particularly cooperative about leaving us daytime signs of their nighttime working: Look for stumps gnawed to a point, dams, mound-like lodges of sticks and mud, brush piles sticking up from water, plunge holes and collapsed tunnels near riverbanks, and "skid road" trails where beavers drag brush to water.

Perhaps the biggest help in spotting animals or their signs is knowing where to look for each species. Your field guide gives you basic information on ranges and preferred habitats.

Thus, in a deep evergreen woods, you know not to waste time looking for ground squirrels. You look for the heaps of cone scales and stripped stems that show a Douglas squirrel has been feeding on the limb above—or you look up in the tree for the little orange-bellied tree squirrel itself.

You know that snags are a good place to look for many birds—for certain flycatchers and hawks that keep a lookout for prey from their bare tops, and for hole-nesting birds from woodpeckers to chickadees that nest in their hollows in spring.

Part of the fun of wildlife watching is learning to see how each species is adapted to the particular kinds of food, cover or other natural protection, and nesting area that it uses. Shorebirds' long legs and bills suit them to wading and probing in mud and shallow water. Soaring hawks have long, broad wings. Hawks that hunt in woods and brush have short wings and long tails for quick braking and maneuvering.

From the fact that animals are so "particular," it follows that the best watching usually is in places with the greatest variety of "niches." You will see far more species where a stream and meadow break the forest than in the evergreen forest itself.

There is no one best technique for watching animals.

A slowly moving car may get you closer to many wild creatures than anything else could. Most animals fear cars much less than they fear people. Even stopped, the car is a good makeshift "blind," especially for photographers who must raise and lower cameras, change lenses, snap shutters, and so on.

But the car has its disadvantages. You don't see things close-up or directly overhead. And bouncing along a dirt road in a stuffy automobile is no way to enjoy the out-of-doors.

Stay away from noisy motorboats and snow-mobiles, unless you are interested only in seeing the rumps of startled, fleeing animals. Canoes, snowshoes, or touring skis are much better.

The pace and flexibility of walking let you savor close-up details, like tracks or wildflowers, and grand vistas like mountains or sunset over the ocean. On a wildlife walk, remember to dress more warmly than you otherwise would: You will spend a lot of time standing still watching. As animals usually are aware of you before you are of them, it usually is best, once you see them, to stay still or approach openly but slowly and with a minimum of excess motion. Sneaking may alarm the animal further. You will soon learn the little flicks of movement that show a particular animal is about to flee. You will get a sense of when to stop, and when to advance again. Some creatures, like chickadees and wrens, are curious and can be "called": They will come closer if you stay still and make a sort of smacking, squeaking sound.

There are special techniques you can use to get to know wildlife that moves at night. Cover a flashlight with red cellophane or fingernail polish. Nocturnal animals do not seem to perceive this light, and you often can watch them in it. Owls often will respond to recordings or imitations of their voices. You can make a "track trap" near your camp. Smooth out a muddy or dusty spot and bait it with some scraps of food. In the morning, tracks will tell you what has been there.

But the nicest way to get to know wildlife may be just sitting still. Some sunny day, pick a likely looking spot—say, a hillside away from trails and roads, where you can look down at brush, a creek, open land, and trees. Sit down with your back to a tree or rock and just wait. Take a nap if you can.

Soon, the land seems to come alive around you. The birds' alarm chirps change back to song. Those that fled return. Chipmunks and squirrels go back to their foraging. Ground squirrels come back out of their burrows. Deer go back to their browsing, looking at you and flicking their tails nervously from time to time.

Something new seems to be happening all the time. New flocks of foraging birds pass through. A hawk soars into view and perches on a snag or plummets down for prey. A coyote trots by.

An hour, two, or three pass before you know it. Sitting still, you can get to know how animals really live: how they feed and keep watch; how they relate to mates, young, and other members of their kind; sometimes how they die. You feel you are a part of this wild world.

A Bit of Wild History

Like human societies, animal kingdoms are invaded, decimated by killing or disease, weakened by changing conditions they cannot adapt to, or strengthened by circumstances they did not create.

Even without man, Washington's wildlife would be changing. But the vast changes in the environment wrought over the past 200 years have left Washington's wild communities abundant and varied, but very different from what they were.

Even before the first whites settled Washington, Indians east of the Cascades acquired horses. Some went wild. There are remnant herds of wild horses in the state today, on the Yakima Indian Reservation.

In the late 18th and early 19th Century era of the fur trade that preceded real settlement, Sea otters were wiped out along most of the Pacific Coast, including Washington. Replanted in the state in 1969, they may be making a small comeback. Beaver, the other local pelt eagerly sought by Hudson's Bay Co. traders, may have become a thoroughly nocturnal animal in this period of heavy persecution by trappers—before a new hat style sent the beaver market crashing.

Settlement, spreading over the state in the late 19th Century, had a devastating effect on many larger mammals.

Grouse at Rainy Pass, North Cascades

The native Roosevelt elk of the Cascades were all but wiped out. (Those you see around Mt. St. Helens probably are a remnant of native stock.) The Columbian white-tailed deer of Western Washington swamps and riverbottoms reached the edge of extinction as the rich soil was cleared and diked to make farms. Sheepmen fought cattlemen for the rangeland of the East Cascades. Their overgrazing wiped out the native tall bunchgrass important to some native animals. And the domestic sheep herds brought scabies. An epidemic of the disease, coming at the same time as heavy hunting and a series of hard winters, is believed to be the reason Washington's native Bighorn sheep virtually disappeared in a few short years.

Hunters as well as grazers were slaughtered. Washington's Grizzly bears and wolves were hunted down, probably to extinction. (Some may survive in the state's northernmost mountains.) Big, shy cougars retreated to the Cascades and Olympics.

Some mammals prospered. Numbers of the native Black-tailed or Mule deer almost certainly increased as farms and clearings were cut in the deep evergreen forest, increasing the greens and brush on which the deer feed. Coyotes probably became more common in Western Washington as more land was cleared.

And some of the losses have been restored. Rocky Mountain elk, introduced to the Cascades early in this Century, may now outnumber the original native herds that roamed from mountains to sea before settlement. Small herds of Bighorn sheep are surviving in the East Cascades and the Blue

Sandhill crane

The Trumpeter swan, largest of North American waterfowl; and the Sandhill crane that trumpets and dances in courtship on the prairies, were big easy targets. And the march of settlement across the continent drained the swamps and prairie potholes where they nested. Both are still rare, in Washington and across the country.

Sage and Sharp-tailed grouse once were common in the semi-desert of Eastern Washington. They strutted and "danced" each year on traditional mating grounds. Irrigation and the plow changed their homeland to farms, and they now are uncommon in the state—although not particularly endangered nationwide.

Some of the changes in Washington were disasters for wildlife—The conversion of miles and miles of the rolling Palouse country in the southeast to wheatfields unbroken by brush creates a virtual wildlife desert.

On the other hand, Western Washington may have more and more varied songbirds since its deep evergreen woods were broken by more fields and brush. The changes make more "niches" where different species can find the food, cover, and nesting habitat they need.

The grain fields, irrigation reservoirs, and seepage lakes man brought to the desert vastly increased the numbers of water-related birds using the area.

Since the 1850s, when Territorial politicians who liked to hunt brought the California quail to Washington, man has been bringing new birds to the state. The Ring-necked pheasant was shipped from the Orient in the 1880s by an Oregon man named consul to China. State game authorities have introduced aliens ranging from Chukar partridges from India to the wild Merriam turkey of the Southwest.

Changes in the state's wildlife have continued into this century. Not all have been clearly due to man. The black-tailed jackrabbit, after spreading slowly west across most of the continent, reached Eastern Washington and took over most of the land that had belonged to the larger native White-tailed jackrabbit. (White-tails still hold the dry mountain edges, with Black-tails in the basin.)

California ground squirrels somehow crossed the Columbia River from Oregon about 1912. They brought a mange that weakened the native Western gray squirrels. And the invaders multiplied faster than the natives. The California ground squirrels now hold much of the former Western gray squirrel territory in the East Cascades.

Chemical pollution has brought changes to Washington wildlife. Peregrine falcons are rare here and nation-wide partly because buildups of DDT caused them to lay eggs with fatally thin

Mountains, as a result of introductions from British Columbia that began in 1957. And the Columbian white-tailed deer finally was given a sizable refuge on the lower Columbia in the 1970s.

Washington's bird populations were affected not just by local events, but by slaughter and waste that went on nation-wide.

To make the big feathered hats fashionable ladies wore into the 20th Century, so many terns and grebes were slaughtered for their white feathers that it was feared they would become extinct. Band-tailed pigeons and many kinds of shorebirds travelled in tight flocks that made easy targets. They, too, were decimated before the nation's first great conservation movement won them protection early in this century. Terns, grebes, and band-tails have made a good recovery. But some of the shorebirds remain rare. One, the Eskimo curlew, is probably extinct.

Less wary species of ducks, and those that nested fairly far south where farms took over their breeding grounds, also suffered. Examples are the Redhead and the Wood duck.

shells. Some suspect that chemical pollution, perhaps of PCBs, another persistent man-made substance, may be causing birth defects and a recent population drop among Puget Sound harbor seals.

But more important than chemical pollution have been simpler, yet almost inevitable results of the spread of man: small boys taking pot-shots at hawks; loons fleeing the lowland lakes where they nested, perhaps because there was just too much disturbance. And the simple loss of habitat as woods and fields become highways and housing tracts.

Man cannot simply decide to leave wildlife alone and let nature take its course. The waterfowl he has encouraged now depend on his crops. Deer, their wild hunters extinct or rare, would multiply to a disastrous stage of mass starvation if man did not hunt them. The elk man has successfully replaced in the Cascades are causing problems by overgrazing parts of Mt. Rainier National Park. And across the state, man and beaver wage a continual war over the beaver's determination to turn suburbs and farms back into beaver ponds.

The only practical choice seems to be continuing to manage wildlife, and doing it better. It is to be hoped that, as more people learn the fascinating variety of the wild world around them, they will try to see to it that we do a better job of stewardship.

Golden-mantled ground squirrel at Cascade Pass

Hoary marmot at Cascade Pass